Only in

OLD

KENTUCKY

Only in OLD KENTUCKY

Historic True Tales of Cultural Ingenuity

Marshall Myers

Charleston · London

THE
History
PRESS

Published by The History Press
Charleston, SC 29403
www.historypress.net

First published 2014

Manufactured in the United States

ISBN 978.1.62619.418.2

Library of Congress CIP data applied for.

I don't want to write about anything else than Kentucky…I want to be steeped in its history, have its people, their characters, their personalities, their modes of life, and thoughts in my brain. This is my plan.

—John Fox Jr.

To my grandsons—Jarrod, Matthew, Ryan, Kurt and Collin—and great-grandson, Eli.

Contents

CONTENTS

Acknowledgements

Any book is not just the product of one person but the effort of many people. This work is no exception. My thanks go to Kirsten Schofield, an editor extraordinaire, for answering my questions and otherwise providing me with expert guidance.

The folks at Information Technology at Eastern Kentucky University, especially Philip Gump, delivered answers to my many inquiries with grace and knowledge.

I also thank Phyllis Bell Conway for taking pictures and being patient as I took pictures.

I want to express my gratitude to all those who helped provide me with images and pictures, including Linda Sizemore.

Thanks go also to *Back Home in Kentucky* magazine, in which many of these stories were first published and whose editors graciously allowed me to use some of the articles in this work.

Lindsey Carr's work on the cover is to be commended, too.

Norma Bowling also provided me with help in the typing and formatting of the text, and Dr. Gill Hunter served as my expert proofreader.

In the end, the book's weaknesses lie with me.

Introduction

Kentucky's culture and history are unique. Few states rival it for its sheer variety of forms and its settlers' ability to so rapidly and cleverly adapt to the environmental and social conditions when they passed through Cumberland Gap to behold what many of its residents even today call paradise.

The settlers came from all over, hearing enticing stories about Kentucky's rich soil, unmatched beauty and plentiful game. Most, however, came from the "Mother State," Virginia, as well as North Carolina and Pennsylvania. But the Scots-Irish, a hard-living and hardworking bunch, soon put their brand on Kentucky life and culture, occupying what was left from those who gobbled up the good land. From the start, the unique blending of the land-hungry aristocrats and the struggling farmers soon led to an interesting mix of those who established profitable plantations and those who had to make do with what they had and what the land would grudgingly give them. The Low Dutch, a group bent on setting up a Dutch colony to maintain their culture and religion, though largely unsuccessful, added their own view of life to the Kentucky landscape.

The Bluegrass Region, with its gently undulating prairie, seemed suited for raising tobacco and, later, hemp, a major crop until the early twentieth century. There, the models from North Carolina and Virginia held sway and slavery flourished, just as it would in the grasslands of far western Kentucky. For some of these first settlers, life was good. The tight caste system inherited from the early men of money provided the "good life" for those often nouveau rich, raising copious crops of hemp and tobacco, worked in large part by slaves. For a time, the moneyed class even practiced the gentleman's art of dueling, following elaborate rules in a time-honored European tradition. Soon, the care and breeding of Kentucky horses led to the state's still-acknowledged equine superiority.

But for much of the rest of the state, the rich farm was gone, leaving sustenance farmers and struggling merchants, particularly the Scots-Irish, to improvise in order to survive. This included making their own gunpowder from the many caves around the state to boiling the saline water that bubbled up across the state in "licks" and supplying themselves with salt for sustenance and preserving meat and various vegetables. Realizing the need for iron for tools, nails and other necessary hardware, this hardy bunch mined the iron-ore deposits to smelt their own iron. They soon adopted methods of preserving pork, in particular, to produce flavorful Kentucky country ham, an often-touted variety unduplicated by rivals in the mountain South.

Along the way, the creative citizens gave their names to various cities and towns across the state. Some were named for coal companies that had established the company-owned towns that predominated life in coal country. Others earned colorful monikers like Black Gnat, Monkey's Eyebrow and Possum Trot, their namers carefully avoiding names of Native Americans who had largely used the Commonwealth as a hunting ground but who were deeply despised by the early settlers who wrestled their land from them.

It is often quite surprising when citizens in other states—whether it be parts of Illinois, Indiana, Missouri, Ohio or various sections of the Deep South—trace their roots and discover Kentucky ancestors, those early settlers from the Commonwealth who transplanted their values, culture and even their language.

The beloved Kentucky poet Jesse Stuart, a devotee of all things Kentucky, once concluded that if the nation is considered a body, Kentucky is its heart. In the minds of many Kentuckians, that is inordinately true.

Chapter 1

Battletown to Berea to Black Gnat: Where Kentuckians Are From

K entuckians who live in places like Possum Trot, Tyewhoppety and Monkey's Eyebrow probably have spent considerable time explaining to others where the places they are from got their names. Such names are so unusual that many people are curious about their origins. Rightly so, since they are so different from spots like Lexington, Newport and Pineville, named for cities elsewhere, prominent people or land features.

Yet overall, the names of places in Kentucky richly reflect the history of the state and its people, often mirroring the residents' own unique pronunciations. Piloted by Robert Rennick's *Kentucky Place Names* and Thomas P. Field's *A Guide to Kentucky Place Names*, with a few exceptions, the Commonwealth's ordinary and extraordinary place names fall into certain categories.

WHY SO FEW NATIVE AMERICAN NAMES?

One of the most interesting things about Kentucky's place names is that so few of them come from the Native Americans who lived there thousands of years before any European Americans ever entered the Bluegrass State. While the state's name and two of its major waterways, the Ohio and Mississippi Rivers, have Native American origins, only one of its largest cities, Paducah, derives from the language of the first people who lived there. In contrast, nearly half of the names of the fifty states have Native American origins, and hundreds of place names in other states reflect these earlier cultures.

Among the few Native American place names in Kentucky are Eskippakithiki, according to Field, a historical spot in Clark County; Eskalapia, the name of a mountain and hollow in Lewis County; and various spellings of Tyewhoppety, which shows up several times in places like Hancock, Hopkins, Owen and Todd Counties, all with uncertain origins. Ouasiota, a gap in Jackson County; Iuka, a town in Livingston County; Ootan, the name of a creek in Caldwell County; and Kuttawa in Lyon County cover most of the names derived from the original residents of Kentucky.

Why so few compared with Tennessee's Tellico, Tullahoma and Etowah or Alabama's Coosa and Talladega Counties or Virginia's Roanoke—states where Native American names are more frequent?

The University of Kentucky's Thomas P. Field, writing some fifty years ago, speculated that he knew why and proposed three main reasons.

First, many of the original names were extremely difficult to pronounce in English. For instance, Wepepocone-Cepewe and Lewekeomi were the Native American names for the Big Sandy River and the Falls of the Ohio at Louisville. These would trip up even the most nimble English tongue.

Second, because of early troubles with the native inhabitants, the early pioneers did not want to name places and rivers after people for whom they had little respect. The few Native Americans these pioneers encountered were their mortal enemies, and the early settlers saw no reason to glorify those people fiercely opposed to settlement of the state.

Third, since there were few permanent aboriginal settlements in the state at the time Europeans settled there, the early settlers set about to name places with familiar words and phrases. Since much of Kentucky, with its abundant supply of game and other foods, became a hunting ground for tribes north and south, pioneers saw few Native Americans compared with other regions of the country. When they did encounter them, the settlers engaged them in bloodletting battles that convinced them that most Native Americans were bloodthirsty savages unworthy of respect and friendship.

SOME NAME PATTERNS

Even without the influence of difficult Native American names, Kentucky still has some rather colorful names. Take, for instance, Sunshine in

Greenup County, Sunrise in Harrison County, Sunnybrook in Wayne County and Brightshade in rural Clay County. Others, like Ordinary in Elliott County, are really extraordinary and include places like Joy in Livingston County, Grab in Green County and Skullbuster in Scott County. City names include New Castle in Henry County, New Concord in Calloway County and New Haven in Nelson—and one place in Owen County is simply named New.

Animals also figure prominently, with spots such as Sunfish in Edmondson County, Panther in Daviess County and Raccoon in Pike County, which goes along with Wild Cat in Clay County and Viper in Perry County, just to cite a few.

A number of small towns have women's names because when many of these hamlets opened their post offices, they had to have a name for the spot. Consequently, postmasters and postmistresses gave them the names of wives and daughters. Hannah in Lawrence County, Virgie in Pike County, Mary Alice in Harlan County, both Nancy and Naomi in Pulaski County and Hazel in Calloway County all illustrate this trend.

One curiosity is that a number of cities that seem as though they should be in a similarly named county are in another. Madisonville, for example, is not in Madison County but in Hopkins County. Likewise, Hopkinsville is not in Hopkins County but rather in Christian County, and Owensboro is not in Owens County but in Daviess County. Or take Campbellsville, which is in Taylor County and not Campbell County. And Clay sits in Webster, not Clay County, while Taylorsville isn't in Taylor but rather Spencer County. Livingston is not in Livingston County but rather Rockcastle County, and even though it may seem logical for Nicholasville to be in Nicholas County, it's actually in nearby Jessamine County.

Many place names in Kentucky are actually the names of countries and cities elsewhere. In the first category are Ireland in Taylor County, Egypt in Jackson County and Cuba in Graves County. In the second group are city names, sometimes spelled slightly differently, from all over the world. These include Bagdad in Shelby, Ghent in Carroll, Manila in Johnson, Berlin in Bracken, London in Laurel, Birmingham in Marshall, Dover in Mason, Glasgow in Barren, Warsaw in Gallatin, Melbourne in Campbell, Bremen in Muhlenberg and Paris in Bourbon County.

Many mistakenly believe that the state's capital is named after the German city with a slightly different spelling. However, its original name was Frank's Ford, named for an early Kentucky pioneer killed near a crossing point on the Kentucky River.

A scattering of biblical names appear on a Kentucky map as well, including Lot in Whitley, Nebo in Hopkins, Ekron in Meade, Berea in Madison and Goshen in Oldham County.

In truth, though, most cities in the state have names that derive either from the names of famous people in the state or outside of it, especially U.S. presidents. Morehead in Rowan County is named for a former governor, as are Shelby County and McCreary County. Washington in Mason County, Madisonville in Hopkins County and Jackson in Breathitt County are all named for presidents, as are Jefferson County and Monroe County. The largest city in the state, Louisville, is named in honor of King Louis XVI of France, who was a strong supporter of the colonies during the Revolutionary War, and Fayette County is named after another Frenchman, Marquis de Lafayette, who aided in that same war.

Heroes of various wars also have spots in the Bluegrass State. Both Hazard and the county in which it is located, Perry County, are named for Oliver Hazard Perry, while Marion County refers to a Revolutionary War hero. Both Daviess County, an altered version of the surname of Colonel Joseph Daveiss, and the largest city in that county, Owensboro, are named for soldiers killed at the Battle of Tippecanoe. Meade County got its name for Captain James Meade, killed at the Battle of River Raisin, which occurred at nearly the same time.

Curiously, a few spots got their names because they are between places. Midway in Woodford County is halfway between Lexington and Frankfort. Another Midway in Crittenden County is halfway between Salem and Marion. Middletown in Jefferson County is supposedly halfway between Louisville and Shelbyville. Halfway in Allen County is supposedly midway between Bowling Green and the Tennessee line, while Center in Metcalfe County is located equidistant from Glasgow, Edmonton, Greensburg and Munfordville.

UNIQUE PRONUNCIATIONS

Kentuckians often give unique pronunciations to the Commonwealth's cities, many times quite different from their original pronunciations. Versailles quickly comes to mind, but some other cities in the state have pronunciations that seem to follow a rule. Generally, to the Kentucky speaker at least, the first syllable in the name often ends in a long vowel (a vowel, generally, that says its name). Kentuckians then stress the first syllable. For instance, with

Fayette County (FAY-ette), originally LaFayette (La-Fay-ETTE), the natives dropped the "La" and stressed the remaining first syllable, giving it a different pronunciation from the original French.

A few other names illustrate this trend. Athens in Fayette County also follows the long vowel rule. Natives stress what they see as the first syllable and say "AY-thens" instead of its usual pronunciation, "ATH-ens." Similarly, it's "HE-bron" for Hebron, "CAY-ro" for Cairo and "YO-se-mite" for Yosemite (rather than yo-SEM-i-te).

Like many other words in the English language, English speakers tend to stress the first syllable. Americans say "DIFF-ere-ence," while the French say "diff-er-ENCE," so it's only natural that place names from other languages would get a different turn in English.

SOME INTERESTING HISTORIES

Finally, Kentucky has many rather unusual names with colorful histories. Following are several examples.

Ono in Russell County, according to Rennick's book, may have received its rather unusual moniker as a result of a public meeting called by members of the community to decide upon a name for the tiny town. According to local lore, each name suggested was met with an, "Oh, no!" So, after every possibility was exhausted, the group finally settled on "Oh, no" but spelled it Ono.

Crummies in Harlan County is not the description of the place or its residents but rather derived from the name of a female bison or deer with a crumpled horn, which the residents then attached to the surrounding community.

Many say that Black Gnat in Taylor County got its name for the thousands of dark bugs that covered a newly painted schoolhouse in the area.

Monroe County's Bugtussle received its unusual name from itinerant wheat thrashers who slept in a nearby barn infested with crawling insects with which they "tussled" all night.

According to legend, Battletown in Meade County got its name when Nathan Hubbard and Jimmy Bennett became engaged in a daylong fight over either where the post office would be or what it would be named.

Boxville in Union County was named when Lincoln Agin built a box-shaped house on the community's land, causing the early residents to give the community the mocking moniker.

The Lee County community of Fixer, according to local lore, was named when postmaster Simon Crabtree became so exasperated after having every name he suggested to the postal authorities turned down that he told them to "fix 'er" themselves.

Possum Trot in Marshall County received its name, so the story goes, as the result of a discussion between possum hunters Sol King and Buck Bolen, one of whom said to the other, "If we don't catch one soon, these possums are going to trot across the road and be gone."

The aforementioned Tyewhoppety in Todd County has a confusing history, with some saying it is a Shawnee word meaning "a place of no return" and others arguing that it means "an unkempt, ill-appearing person."

And then there is Monkey's Eyebrow in Ballard County. While still debated, the name probably refers to a nearby brush-covered hill that gave the appearance, when seen from a distance, of a monkey's eyebrow.

Many more interesting names with unusual histories dot a map of the Commonwealth. Thomas P. Field concludes that the early residents "proceeded to name the physical and cultural features of their habitat in a distinctly American manner" that, at times, veered toward the unusual.

But if you're in Awe, ready to spend some Hardmoney and do some Fairdealing while wearing a Hi Hat as a Habit but still Needmore cash, you could end up in Prosperity or in Poverty—and the whole time, you'd be in Kentucky.

Chapter 2

Company Towns or Coal Camps:
What Loretta Lynn and Tennessee Ernie Ford
Sang About

In many places, all that's left is a rusty pipe jutting out of the ground, one jonquil that blooms regularly every spring or maybe a half-buried gnarled old work shoe with the laces gone.

Not too long ago, though, these weed-covered spots, now frequently forgotten, teemed with life: children playing in the fenced-in yards; gardens growing with corn, beans, onions, radishes and all kinds of vegetables; automobiles, some with running boards, covered with a black, gritty dust; clotheslines with whites and coloreds flapping in the breeze and grey shirts bouncing in time to a gentle wind; front porches with swings creaking in the back-and-forth rhythms of occupants sharing the latest neighborly news; and the sweet smell of supper—soup beans cooked with a ham hock and fried potatoes, cornbread smeared with butter and a steaming blackberry cobbler in season, an aroma so inviting that most didn't have to be called twice to supper.

But now these places are gone; these company towns, sometimes called coal camps, are all just distant and fading memories—both good and bad—in the minds of older folks. But in their time, scores of company towns flourished in the coal-mining regions of the eastern Kentucky mountains and the rolling hills and coal fields of western Kentucky. They were called company towns simply because the coal company owned everything: the homes, the school, the meeting center, the company store and, sometimes, even the garden plots. Rent was cheap and taken out of the workers' pay.

What Were Company Towns Like?

The houses, usually wood-framed or stucco structures, were often alike. One study, the Boone Report, described the typical company town as having "monotonous rows of houses and privies, all in the same faded hues, standing alongside the railroad tracks close to a foul creek; or camps like ones farther up the valley, with scattered houses on stilts, perilously perching there, with their privies behind them on steep hillsides."

These towns were gritty, workingman places, with laborers trudging home at the end of their shifts with coal dust–smeared faces and scratched and dented hard hats—no suits and ties, except maybe at the Sunday church service. Country music stars Loretta Lynn and Tennessee Ernie Ford have sung about company towns, so interwoven into the fabric of southern culture were they.

But often the residents who lived in company towns didn't see them as the drab, dreary places the Boone Report describes. Three former residents of coal camps, quoted in Crandall Shifflett's *Coal Towns*, described their houses in a different way. "[They were] real nice," one former resident recalled. "They kept them [the houses] up. They painted them about every two or three years." In fact, "You had to keep it nice; you couldn't let your yard get messed up. If you did, they [the company] sent a man around to clean it up and then made you pay for it. I liked that part about it because nobody could let their yards…get messed up, like some of them now."

In Oolite, Kentucky, a company town I once called home, all the houses had three to four bedrooms and were grey stucco or wood-framed structures with modern plumbing, differing only slightly from each other, some with neatly manicured yards.

Thomas Keleman's history of Lynch records that the town had concrete sidewalks, curbs and gutters with rear porches, as well as a concrete highway. Yet other coal camps were squalid places, often characterized by unkempt houses on stilts, outdoor privies, muddy streets and few features that would make a miner feel proud to live there. Keleman notes that many company towns were often segregated settlements with separate sections for Eastern Europeans, Italians and African Americans, a practice in the spirit of the times, especially in the South.

Keleman concludes that "coal camps varied from one extreme to the other. Like the mining operations, some were planned, well-financed, and well-managed ventures, while others were worse than miserable. Most lay somewhere between these two extremes."

Studying company housing in the coal camps, economist Price Fishback found that in Kentucky, a whopping 70 percent of the coal companies furnished housing for their workers. The advantages of providing such housing are obvious. Having workers within a few yards of their work promoted a sense of loyalty within the workers; after all, the laborers were literally a part of the company. Another advantage for the company was that the employee and his family would shop at the company store, often but not always resulting in huge profit for the company.

Many would believe that companies charged exorbitant monthly rent for the houses. But that's not what Fishback found. In fact, he notes that the monthly rent was often less than that charged by landlords outside the town. After all, the company had a stake in keeping workers housed in its town. Companies surely knew that charging higher rent would immediately be met with demands for higher wages, and keeping wages down and keeping workers well housed surely affected the company's bottom line.

To offset utility costs, the company charged residents for these services, and Fishback found that these charges were often less than those in outside communities. However, residents sometimes had deductions from their paychecks for the costs of a company doctor and even for a funeral fund if the company had one.

Some considered a company town a good place in which to grow up because there were like-minded people, livable wages, good schools and steady, lifetime employment. As Loretta Lynn says in her song "Coal Miner's Daughter," "I never thought of leaving Butcher Holler." Yet still others felt strongly that the company towns allowed the company to meddle too much in the residents' business, often controlling virtually every aspect of their lives. Workers felt trapped by the big bosses in Chicago or New York, people who, to these workers at least, didn't really care about the little man slaving away in some dark dungeon, giving his sweat and suffering from an aching back just so that the owners could drink their champagne and eat filet mignon in exclusive, candle-lit restaurants.

The big owners were large corporations like U.S. Steel, Consolidated Coal Company, International Harvester and United States Coal Company—industries that in one way or another used or supplied coal in the manufacturing process and that felt little guilt in asking a miner and his family to leave if he were laid off or killed or quit.

SOME UNIQUE ASPECTS OF COMPANY TOWNS

While company towns differed in minor ways from each other, most were clearly marked by aspects that set them apart from the tiny towns and villages that dot the Kentucky landscape. Company towns were places that left their

A typical company store. *Library of Congress.*

mark on those who worked or grew up there. These people had memories not just of the community itself but also of the schools and the company store.

On average, the schools built by the company were much better funded than those on the outside since the company either paid the entire salary of the teachers or at least supplemented their salaries, making them plumb assignments for teachers. In Oolite, the gray stucco school building had a coal furnace, stoked daily in the winter by the eighth-grade boys, and flush toilets that used Ohio River water. This was in contrast to almost all the one-room schools in the county, which typically had to settle for outhouses. Although we had to carry our drinking water from a well up through the valley, the schoolyard was ample in size and regularly mowed by the company's personnel. We had enough space for softball and dodge ball games, limited only by the river on one side and tall hills on the other.

Some company towns boasted even more elaborate buildings, with gymnasiums and well-equipped facilities that provided proper atmospheres for young scholars from the coal camps, and furnished meeting places for school and community activities like cake walks, box suppers and other recreational activities.

According to Shifflett, while some mining camps were large enough to contain commissaries, where miners could buy clothing and food, most mining communities were not big enough to have these elaborate shopping facilities. These communities had to turn elsewhere.

Perhaps the most famous (and infamous) building in company towns was the company store, often maligned by both outsiders and residents. Tennessee Ernie Ford's 1950s song "Sixteen Tons" contains the line, "I owe my soul to the company store," sung with a deep moan reflecting the pent-up feelings some miners felt about their local general store.

But were the company stores really as bad as their reputation makes them out to be? The answer to that question rests upon just what the company store was in that particular company town. Some stores were ruthless attempts to get as much money as they could out of the patrons; others weren't quite that bad.

SCRIP, FLICKERS AND CLACKERS

In some cases, until the passage of various state laws, the company store accepted only scrip, sometimes called clackers, stickers, flickers or chink-tin, among other names. Scrip was a substitute for cash issued by the company and paid to the workers. Some scrip was made of aluminum, brass or even paper, but all scrip had the reputation of being worth less than hard money, especially when it could be redeemed only at the company store.

Since many coal camps were in isolated communities far from the nearest town, the company had workers in a vise. If they needed groceries and their scrip was redeemable only at the company store, and the nearest commercial grocery was miles away and largely inaccessible most of the year, then miners often were left with no other choice but to redeem their scrip at the company store. One authority on scrip, John Freddie Wilson, notes that sometimes scrip was worth as little as fifty cents on the dollar, with other scrip redeemable at eighty to eighty-five cents. To make it even worse, rarely was scrip acceptable outside the company town.

What made payment in scrip particularly onerous was that when a miner wanted an advance on his pay, he was often paid again in scrip. On occasions, then, a miner drew little or no pay on payday, leaving him deeply in debt to the company store.

But the Coal Commission concluded that the prices at company stores "were similar to prices at nearby independent stores. Prices apparently were higher at isolated mines, in part due to higher transportation costs, but scattered evidence suggests that higher prices were partially offset by higher wages," although the experiences of many miners often disputed that claim.

In addition to groceries, company stores sold a variety of other items a mining family would need, including sewing notions, patent medicine and some clothing. If the company store didn't have the item the family wanted, many used mail-order houses like Sears and Roebuck, Montgomery Ward and other companies specializing in trading through the mail. Loretta Lynn sings about getting the family shoes through "a mail-order catalog." Families unsure of a shoe size used a pencil to draw the outline of a foot on a piece of paper, enclosed it with their mail order and anxiously waited several weeks for the package to arrive. A new pair of shoes, sometimes worn only in winter, was like an early Christmas. The merchandise was often delivered to the company store since it usually served as the post office, too.

But besides being a spot where the miners traded, the company store was also a gathering place where families could pick up their mail, swap stories with their neighbors about the sick and shut-ins and even wile away the end of a long, hard day while sipping on a Pepsi flavored with a nickel bag of salted peanuts.

In Oolite, the company store was one of the few places with a television set. Here, residents could stare at the big, snowy eye as politicians vied for votes or two wrestlers contorted each other into a variety of holds. Each Friday night, all gathered at the store, awaiting the grocery truck to wind through the hills and unload some surprises such as toy cars, dolls or a fresh jar of pickled boloney.

WHY THEY DISAPPEARED

By the 1960s, the company town began disappearing. A combination of reasons might explain why these communities were abandoned. Some say the unionization of miners soured the relationship between the parent company and the miners to the point that the company and miners no longer cared about living in a company-owned town. Others say that with improved roads, miners began buying automobiles and preferred to live the American Dream and buy their own homes. Still others cite the advent of sophisticated mining equipment that required fewer and fewer men

The coal camp of Jenkins, Kentucky. *Used with permission of Roger Philpot, author of* Kentucky Coal Mining.

to operate, significantly cutting back the need for so many miners. And a few say the demand for coal from Kentucky, with its high sulphur content, sharply declined, resulting in the need for considerably fewer miners. In the end, some company towns, like Lynch and Jenkins, gradually were bought from the company, and homeowners replaced what at one time had been a company town.

Loretta Lynn says of Butcher Holler, "Nothing's left but the floor/Nobody lives here anymore/Except the memories of a coal miner's daughter." In many ways, her words are accurate, for company towns have gone the way of penny candy, thirty-cent gasoline and trucks with running boards. But in their time, for good or bad, they were vibrant communities where people lived, loved and, all too often, died—the memories of them and the town fading into the past like smoke from a coal-burning stove, weaving its way out of a grey mountain valley.

Chapter 3

To Teach and to Learn:
Settlement Schools in Eastern Kentucky

THE FOUNDERS

In the last quarter of the nineteenth century in the United States (the "Gilded Age," as Mark Twain called it), much of the stage belonged to the "robber barons"—men like Andrew Carnegie, J.P. Morgan, Jay Gould, Cornelius Vanderbilt and John D. Rockefeller. It was a time when men with money predominated not just the culture of the times but even tried their hands at influencing the government itself. Many citizens felt that this small group of "robber barons" preyed on the ordinary man to accumulate their great hordes of gold.

But the years that followed were times when the rich and even the super rich looked to do more than just accumulate stacks of money. Andrew Carnegie, for instance, built libraries across the country. Vanderbilt and Carnegie contributed to higher education by giving generously to schools that still bear their names. Such philanthropy led to the appearance that these moneyed men were generously giving back to American society, whether that was true or not.

In addition to these men, a large number of people, especially women with a New England education from places like Vassar, Smith College and Mount Holyoke, began to think about giving back, too. These young and often idealistic women, the daughters of men who had earned their substantial means from big industry and the financial markets, joined a crusade called the Progressive Movement.

In particular, these women began to think more seriously about how to improve the lives of all citizens of the country. Their many causes encompassed a concern about the plight of the poor, the most effective ways government could improve the lives of all of its citizens, involving more people in the political process, weeding out corruption in politics, women's suffrage, teaching the fundamentals of healthy living and literacy. It was to them an age of optimism, and they were firm in their belief that their quality educations equipped them to revolutionize life in the United States. Articulated by leaders like Walter Rauschenbusch, the Social Gospel, the challenge that churches ought to be involved in improving the lives of the poor, became to them an additional theological impetus for the work of many progressives.

One aspect of the Progressive Movement was the establishment of settlement houses, frequently located in poor, urban, mixed-ethnic neighborhoods. The first settlement house was Hull House in Chicago, founded by Jane Addams and Ellen Gates Starr. The establishment's purpose was to provide what the two women considered essentials to a happy and healthy life—the basics of nutrition, education, the arts and child rearing— to the many immigrants and the underprivileged.

As the Progressive Movement spread across the country, including centers of population and wealth in Lexington and Louisville, several young, single women from well-to-do families, many from New England, began missionary work in the mountains of Appalachia, including eastern Kentucky. While most of these women were from Protestant denominations, Roman Catholics also made legitimate efforts in the region.

Many of these reformers had been lured to the region by stories about the residents published in the numerous popular magazines of the era. Ron Eller, in his book *Miners, Millhands, and Mountaineers*, observes that "between 1870 and 1890 over two hundred travel accounts and short stories were published in which mountain people emerged as a rude, backward, romantic, and sometimes violent race who had quietly lived for generations in isolation from the mainstream of American life." In fact, many of the demeaning stereotypes that still exist about Appalachian people owe their existence to these early writers.

THEY DEFINE THEIR MISSION

While early reformers quickly realized the gross inaccuracies written about mountain life, they soon concluded that more needed to be done in this region than just a few short-lived missions. In their minds, many residents of this largely isolated section of Kentucky lagged far behind the rest of the country in the essentials of modern living. As these privileged women saw it, these locals needed help. They needed nurses, teachers and other forms of medical aid; churches to instill ethics to prevent the many and constant feuds so much a part of mountain life; help in developing ways of earning a living that didn't depend just on the tiny hillside farms; and more education than what the scattered and, many times, inadequate one-room schools could provide.

Writing about the role of these women, Betty Parker Duff, who studies the settlement movement, quotes a Presbyterian minister from Hazard who wrote to a women's organization asking for women "to assist in the conduct of meetings of wives, mothers, housekeepers, young ladies and little girls. Lessons and lectures in cooking and homemaking should be made particularly enthusiastic and then the intellectual and moral features can be made interesting."

That's not to say that men were left out. Karen Tice, a scholar of the region, quotes a mountaineer who saw his own land and people as "lost from knowledge," noting that "too many mountain people were not even taught up as to morality." He went on to say that there was "lots of whiskey and wickedness," where the older generation had "laid the pattern for drinking, killing, whoring, and abomination in the sight of God."

Not surprisingly, the mountain people found many of these reform-minded women who came to the mountain to be quite "quare"; that is, they wondered why these single women were not married. Or they referred to the young ladies as "fetched-on," women who exhibited some rather peculiar ways to these mountaineers since these different ways frequently ran counter to their culture.

But as mountaineers began to realize that these "quare" women were, for the most part, sincere in their desire to help the locals live healthier and richer lives, their distrust began melting away. At the same time, the reformers also began to understand that some of the mountain culture needed saving.

While other issues such as health and nutrition also received attention, one thing became quite obvious: the region needed good schools to educate not only the children but also adults who wanted to learn to read and learn basic mathematics—knowledge that would very quickly enrich their lives.

EARLY SETTLEMENT SCHOOLS

In other parts of Appalachia, schools were later established in the mountains of Georgia, North Carolina and Virginia—some two hundred schools in all. But Hindman Settlement School in Knott County, Kentucky, was, according to the *Kentucky Encyclopedia*, "the first rural settlement school in the United States."

Many residents of this particular region clearly saw the need for such a place. Uncle Solomon Everidge told one of the founders, "While I was just a chunk of a boy hoeing corn on the steep mountain side, when I'd get to the end of the row, I would look up Troublesome Creek and down Troublesome Creek and wonder if anyone would ever come in to learn us anything. But nobody ever came in and nobody ever went out; so we just growed up and never knowed nuthin'. I can't read or write, but I have children, greats and grands, and I want them to have a chance for larnin'."

Unlike many settlement schools, Hindman Settlement School in Knott County was nondenominational, the product of the work of Kentuckians Katherine Pettit and Mary Stone, who received support from the Kentucky Federation of Women's Clubs, the Women's Temperance Union, various charitable organizations and wealthy patrons.

From the beginning, Hindman Settlement School was a very special place. With many students boarding, often earning their keep by working on the school's farm, the school promised a quality and rigorous education while also serving the needs of the community by offering health services, help with agriculture, a meeting place for the local community and developing cottage industries that marketed local crafts.

Music historian Virginia Chambers says that one phase of mountain life that proved to be a surprisingly rich well of interest was the indigenous music of the area. Pettit often traveled to various places in the mountains, collecting age-old ballads like "Pretty Polly," "Lord Daniel's Wife" and "The Drunkard's Dream," and she heard similar songs from her students. Soon, music lovers from outside the region roamed the mountains, recording ditties often transported to the mountains by the early Irish and English settlers. The music included rich deposits of ballads and songs frequently thought to have been long lost over the years elsewhere.

Chambers concludes that by showing a sincere interest in the music of the region, Pettit formed a tight bond with the locals. The local residents felt that their culture did indeed have value to not only them but also to educated people from outside, who evidenced a keen and abiding interest in the musical heritage of the mountains.

Pine Mountain Settlement School, one of several settlement schools in eastern Kentucky. *Courtesy of the Kentucky Historical Society.*

In his history of the school, Jess Stoddart sums up the total work of Pettit and Stone at the school: "They taught; they learned; they found themselves part of an exciting and satisfying cultural exchange. Over time, they became important and influential leaders in the world of mountain reform."

A sister institution of Hindman Settlement School was Pine Mountain School in Harlan County. Founded by the same Katherine Pettit, along with Ethel de Long, the school also focused on educating mountain youngsters. And in borrowing an idea from its neighbor, the schoolwork often emphasized serving the community while attempting to meet the needs of the individual students from that area.

Frequently modeling themselves after Hindman Settlement, other settlement schools soon followed, prompted at times by events in the mountains that many residents could no longer tolerate. One such school was Henderson Settlement School in the Laurel Fork Valley. A Methodist minister, Reverend Hiram Frakes, witnessed a murder trial in which key witnesses failed to testify against the alleged perpetrators for fear of reprisal. Motivated to change conditions in the community, Frakes sought help from his bishop to found a school.

His request fell on sympathetic ears. Hearing of Frakes's mission, Bertha Bell, from a training school, volunteered to be the school's first teacher, and local residents Scott Partin and Bill Henderson donated a generous amount of land upon which to build the campus. Soon, a church was constructed, and in the 1930s, Reverend Frakes turned part of the school's land into a farm, a gristmill and a sawmill—all designed to help keep the schoolhouse doors open. In addition, the Methodist Board of Missions and churches far away from the school underwrote the salaries of the teacher and supplied clothing and toys to the young scholars at Henderson Settlement. To raise money and gain publicity for their cause, Frakes organized a quartet of singers called the Sunbonnet Girls, who traveled far and ended up singing for President Herbert Hoover in the White House.

THE BIRTH OF ALICE LLOYD COLLEGE

One college in eastern Kentucky began as Caney Creek Community Center in Knott County, founded by a Bostonian named Alice Lloyd, a graduate of Radcliffe College. With much of the same mission as other settlement schools, the original grounds soon evolved from Caney Creek High School to Caney Creek Junior College and in 1981 settled into Alice Lloyd College. The historian of the college, P. David Searles, says, "For seventy years [Alice Lloyd College and its predecessors] has enabled thousands of students from Appalachia to obtain a college education at little or no cost."

Today, Alice Lloyd College enrolls about six hundred students. Assisted in her work by June Buchanan, early on, Alice Lloyd held definite ideas about what she wanted her graduates to look like, and her influence is still felt today. To her credit, she realized that the college's mission was ultimately to aid the community itself. As Searles notes, about 75 percent of the graduates have stayed in the mountains to serve their respective areas, a figure indicative of Lloyd's success.

According to the *Encyclopedia of Appalachia*, other settlement schools in the state include Lotts Creek Community School, Redbird Mission School, Stuart Robinson School and Kingdom Come School.

By contrast, Roman Catholic settlement schools, such as St. Theresa School in Lee County and St. Cecilia School in Perry County, were founded by nuns, priests and brothers—not by lay people as the protestant schools generally were. These Catholic schools performed many of the same functions as other settlement schools and were aimed at bettering the lives of those in the community they served by providing clothing and medical attention. Like other settlement schools, these places of learning were funded by philanthropists from the urban centers of the East Coast.

As the state of Kentucky provided more and more for the educational needs of the children in eastern Kentucky, the days of the settlement schools with their emphases on education and community service have passed. But two schools continue to have the community in mind, only with different emphases. Today, Hindman Settlement School treats children with dyslexia, serves as place for local artisans to meet and acts as a bucolic meeting place for writers. Pine Mountain School, conscious of the damage of various coal mining operations, has become a center for educating the community on environmental issues.

While Appalachian historians at times disagree about the effects settlement schools had on life in the eastern Kentucky mountains, one student of the region's history, Henry Hinkle, says that "the settlement schools and the services they provided were strong influences on the people and culture of their communities. Loyal and vocal supporters… speak of their times at the settlement schools as some of the best and most important [times] of their lives."

Strong testimony any way you look at it.

Chapter 4

The Low Dutch Settlements in Kentucky: Stories of Brave and Determined People

The early European settlers of the United States included a number of ethnic groups who wanted someplace where they could practice their unique form of Christianity and their own brand of European culture. In particular, the Quakers in Pennsylvania and the Puritans in Massachusetts come to mind as representatives of those groups—two among many.

But one group, instrumental in settling New York and surrounding states, chose frontier Kentucky as the place to found a colony, a colony where they could celebrate their heritage and preach their own strain of Calvinism. This group, who referred to themselves as "Low Dutch," had been pushed out of Manhattan and surrounding areas by the land-hungry English until "New Amsterdam," named for the Dutch city, became "New York," named for the English city, leaving the Low Dutch there to live under the authority of the British Crown.

But not before the Low Dutch had left their imprint on American culture. Even today, we bake "Dutch apple pies," "go Dutch treat" when funds for a date run low, give "Dutch uncle" talks to those needing advice directly delivered, find ourselves "in Dutch" when we break some social convention or eat "waffles," "cranberries," "coleslaw" and "crullers," just to name a few words that originated in the Low Dutch culture and language.

By the latter years of the 1700s, many Low Dutch had settled in rural Pennsylvania at a place called Conewago, close to Gettysburg. Yet according to Vincent Aker's extended and most complete study of their history, they still burned with the desire to have their own colony away from the influence of other groups. Some, in fact, had caught "Kentucky Fever," like so many other people. After all, the stories told about a place where the game was plentiful, providing countless opportunities for fur trading; the soil was rich; and the many springs, creeks and rivers meant easy access to markets outside of Kentucky. And best of all, land was cheap and unsettled.

At last they would have the chance to found a colony where they would be left alone and prosper together, away from the nagging influence of other groups. It wasn't that they were unfriendly or hostile; it was simply a longing to be with their own kind. As Akers notes, their purpose was simple: as a group, they would all gather together, move to largely unsettled Kentucky and buy a rich parcel of land large enough so that not just only their generation but also future generations would have a colony all their own.

THE LURE OF THE BLUEGRASS STATE

At first, a few moved west into the hill country of what is now called Berkeley County, West Virginia—a sparsely settled area at the time—but the isolation only intensified the lure that Kentucky had for many of them. But could the Low Dutch believe all the stories about the bounty and beauty of Kentucky? To answer that and other questions, Samuel Duree, along with eight other Low Dutch settlers and two African Americans, left their homes, set their eyes westward and crossed the steep mountains of Appalachia into the Bluegrass State. Following the Wilderness Road through Cumberland Gap, they arrived at Boonesborough on April 7, 1779, the fort protecting them and the settlers already there from hostile Indians. The Indians thought, quite frankly, that this was their hunting territory, as it had been for generations, and didn't have much patience with those white settlers occupying their land.

THE NATIVE AMERICANS DEFEND THEIR LAND

At this point in their frontier experience, however, the Low Dutch did not fully appreciate the extent of the problems settlers were having with marauding Indians. In fact, just before arriving at Boonesborough, Akers relates that the Low Dutch party under Duree, through sheer good fortune, escaped Indian attack. Another party under a Captain Starms had left

Boonesborough headed in the opposite direction, east toward Virginia. The Indians in the area had quickly picked up the trail of the group and later nearly wiped out the entire party, leaving only a few survivors.

But just by chance, the Indians and Starms's men had somehow missed the Duree party headed west toward Fort Booneborough when the group had temporarily rambled off the road, only to discover when they found the trail again that an Indian party was following what they later learned was the Starms group, heading in the opposite direction.

Now alert that Indians were in the immediate vicinity, and with six miles to the safety of the fort, Duree and his men decided to stop for the night. One member proposed that they get off the trail again and sleep without a fire, which would likely alert Indians in the region of the party's whereabouts. But one member, a Calvinist to the core, convinced the group that if it were their time to die, there really wasn't much they could do about it anyway.

So they built a large, roaring fire and settled down for the night. Upon seeing the blaze, the Indians thought that Duree's party was pulling some kind of trick—surely the Duree group had more sense than to start a fire with the enemy all around. So the Native Americans stole away, believing that the fire was a ruse, leaving Duree and his men unharmed. It was one of the few times that the Low Dutch would be so lucky. But they saw their narrow escape as a sign indeed from God that Kentucky was where they should settle.

Since the Low Dutch party wanted to find out more about Kentucky, a few days later, a group of men set out from the fort to see what the countryside was like. The nine men soon happened upon Muddy Creek and some of its tributaries in eastern Madison County. One of the men, Samuel Duree, saw possibilities for a millrace on Muddy Creek, but the eight others envisioned meager potential for this section of land.

At any rate, the Low Dutch party as a whole reported back to the two groups in Berkeley County and Conewago. Their assessment of the landscape must have been favorable, for the two separate groups then set out for Kentucky via two routes.

The families from Berkeley, thirty people in all, traveled the Wilderness Road through the Cumberland Gap and arrived at White Oak Springs Station about a half mile above Fort Boonesborough in March of 1780 but suffered one fatality when David Banta was killed en route.

The other group from Conewago, about seventy-five in all, including a large number of children, took the Ohio River route, arriving at what is now the Louisville area about the same time as the Berkeley party. Led by Henry

Banta, the Pennsylvanians established Low Dutch Station, part of six other stations near Beargrass Creek in eastern Jefferson County on a trail now known as Dutchman's Lane.

But, as Akers records, the Low Dutch there were hardly satisfied with living on Beargrass Creek, especially after hearing repeated stories about fertile land in other parts of central Kentucky. As a result, by the summer of 1780, John and Christopher Westerfield and an accompanying party headed south to Fort Harrod in present-day Harrodsburg, Mercer County.

Along the way, Akers says, at about three o'clock in the morning, John Thickston, the scout they had hired, was startled out of his sleep to find three Indians inspecting his gun. Instinctively, Thickston jerked the gun from one of the Indians. The Indian lifted his tomahawk high to strike Thickston a mortal blow.

But Thickston managed to hit the attacker with the butt of his gun, knocking the Indian down just long enough for Thickston to hurry toward the safety of darkness. Yet amidst the gunfire, Thickston suffered a gunshot wound to the neck. Shaking it off, he scurried into the darkness until he stumbled over a log.

When Thickston turned around, he saw the Indians frantically throwing saddles and anything else that would stoke the fire and render more light. Then he heard the desperate shrieks from his party as they were being attacked and the awful, dull thud of tomahawks splitting skulls.

John and Christopher Westerfield and two others were slain, but the women and children were captured and taken to the British in Detroit. Two others, one in the throes of a seizure and another wounded woman, seemed too much trouble to the fleeing Indians and were summarily tomahawked to death.

Yet the Low Dutch would not be deterred.

After harvesting their crops, in February 1781, sixteen Low Dutch settlers left the safety of the Beargrass Station, headed for Muddy Creek in Madison County near Duree's mill. After about forty days there, near present-day Moberly, Peter Duree and John Bullock brought their families to the area.

Three days later, Indians attacked. For their safety, the families holed up in a cabin, but when the two men left the house to find something to make more corn meal, both were killed. And when Mrs. Bullock ran out to aid her husband, she was slain, too. That left only Mrs. Duree to fend off the attackers. Frantically, she grabbed a gun and moved from one gun hole in the cabin to another, again and again, ultimately confusing the Indians, who shortly left the area. Those Low Dutch remaining returned to safety to the Low Dutch Station on Beargrass Creek.

In the summer of that same year, nine Low Dutchmen decided to set out for Estill Station, three miles southeast of present-day Richmond, to see the tillable land that one of the Low Dutch settlers, Abraham Banta, had rented from Captain James Estill. The group's intent was to rescue tools that the Low Dutch had used building cabins the winter before.

According to Abraham Banta's *Conquest of a Continent: Nine Generations in the American Frontier*, Captain James Estill was riding point while his brother Sam was pulling up the rear. About a half mile from Estill's Station, the group, following Lick Trace, came upon a felled red oak tree blocking the path. The oak, they soon learned, had been chopped down by Indians with ambush on their minds.

The Indians lay hidden behind the tree as the party neared, camouflaged by leaves and limbs. But as the party of nine neared the tree, Sam Estill spied a moccasin amid all the greenery. He shouted, "Indians!" before firing his rifle in the direction of the moccasin, jumping off his horse and scurrying for cover.

The Indians fired back, striking Captain Estill in the arm and shattering the bone. Then his horse panicked and galloped back toward Estill Station; Captain Estill hung on desperately to the reins, but he was unable to stop the frightened animal.

As the battle ensued, an enormous Indian, painted black and armed with a tomahawk, jumped from his position in the tree, aiming a tomahawk at Frederick Ripperdan's skull. Scared to helplessness, Ripperdan bellowed to Sam Estill, "Shoot the son of a *****!"

Sam Estill shouted back, "Why don't you shoot him yourself? Your gun is loaded, while mine is empty!"

Ripperdan raised his gun to his shoulder and fired, the musket nearly touching the ferocious Indian's chest. The Indian fell slowly, hopelessly hanging onto a sapling for support while his tomahawk slowly slipped to the ground. Passing from the Indian's dying lips was a deep and desperate groan that sounded "like a bear's roar."

Scared, the rest of the Indians quickly fled.

The Low Dutch settlers termed the skirmish the "Dutch Defeat," their way of saying that they had given up on settling in Madison County.

Many of those who farmed near Fort Boonesborough then sought safety in Mercer County along with other Low Dutch settlers. Yet they intended to stay in Mercer County only temporarily until they had acquired enough land for their colony.

According to Akers, in 1782, discouraged by Indian troubles and tired of living in crowded conditions in Mercer County and elsewhere, the Low

Dutch decided to take their case to the Continental Congress. Maybe if the Low Dutch made a good enough argument, these early lawmakers could help them fulfill their dreams. So 105 of them signed a petition in which they spelled out their purpose: "to procure a Tract of Land to enable them to settle together in a body for the conveniency of civil society and propagate the Gospel in their known language."

Presently, they argued, they had to live in "such a distressed and confined way, always in danger, frequently on military duty" that they found it "impossible for them to do more than barely support their families with the necessities of life."

Like so many other Kentucky pioneers, the Low Dutch settlers said that much of the land in Kentucky was tied up by "memorialists" who had laid claim to "all the tillable land," making it impossible to acquire the acreage they needed.

In truth, the Low Dutch seemed to have said all the right things that would support their case, but the Continental Congress was not willing to help them until they completed "their general arrangements as to the ceded land."

Still, the Low Dutch were not willing to give up.

Squire Boone and a Land Offer

Somehow, some of the settlers had met Daniel Boone's brother, Squire, who had a treasury warrant from the Commonwealth of Virginia for a tract of land he was willing to sell. Akers says the agreement, negotiated by Abraham Banta, was signed on March 13, 1786, and eventually included the purchase of about 7,610 acres in present-day Henry and Shelby Counties, after further negotiations settled all other claims for the land.

The dream of a Low Dutch colony seemed to have come true. The following day, anxious to get started, the participants immediately drew up a constitution and measured off thirty-four two-hundred-acre plots for those Low Dutch who would settle there.

But almost immediately, the Indians again began making trouble for these early settlers. For instance, when the Indians attacked the Low Dutch settlers near Hogland's Station, the Low Dutch fighters dispatched young Jake Banta to get help from those Low Dutch living in Mercer County. Even though he traveled at night, the Indians soon found him. One buried his tomahawk into Banta's skull and then proceeded to hack at his lifeless flesh in a ferocious and ghastly attack.

In February 1786, Akers notes, a few more Low Dutch left Mercer County and headed for the colony, but Indian attacks in the area continued unabated. In May 1790, Indians killed a group headed by Matthew Smock. Later, in August, Daniel Corzine, a twelve-year-old, was slain by Indians, leaving many well-established Low Dutch in Mercer County leery of leaving the safe confines there for the colony. Yet a few brave settlers settled on the Low Dutch Tract, occupying some of the thirty-four two-hundred-acre tracts.

But to many, "Kentucky was just passing through." So by the second decade of the nineteenth century, many families living on the Low Dutch Tract and those still left in Mercer County were drawn north to new land in Johnson and Switzerland Counties in Indiana, leaving Kentucky behind them.

A Dream Fulfilled?

The Low Dutch dream of having their own unique colony had only partially come true. They had been unsuccessful in attracting a Dutch Reform minister. Many had left the Dutch Reform Church and converted to Presbyterianism. Some Dutch remained in Mercer County, and indeed some settled in the Shelby-Henry Counties area. Yet the dream of a large Low Dutch colony, with families living together, worshiping together and sharing the same language and culture on the Low Dutch Tract, was never fully realized—in spite of the efforts of so many, some of whom had lost their lives for the cause during the seemingly constant trouble with Native Americans. However, many of their proud descendants now live in those places where the Low Dutch pioneers had originally settled, reminding us of their great courage and deep commitment to settle frontier Kentucky.

Chapter 5
When Rowan County Was at War with Itself

As far as nineteenth-century Kentucky feuds go, the Rowan County War (sometimes called the Martin-Tolliver feud) was indeed quite colorful—especially if the color is blood red.

While exact figures are not available, the Rowan County War sent at least twenty people to the graveyard, and probably more if a strict accounting were given. Most sources list this murderous fray as the bloodiest of all Kentucky feuds, bloodier even than the more famous Hatfield-McCoy feud.

At its height, lawlessness was so tightly woven into the very fiber of the county and so out of control that legislators in Frankfort actually considered dissolving the county and sending its parts back to Fleming and Morgan Counties, its original owners. For at the feud's height, Morehead, the county seat, went from a population of about 700 in 1885 to only 296 a mere two years later. Decent, fearful folks scurried to other counties and states to escape the corruption and violence. Even two visits from the state militia could contain the violence only while the soldiers were there, as mayhem reared its ugly and sanguine head as soon as the soldiers were out of the county.

What happened in Rowan County that it could be so aptly described as a "war"? What led to the butchering of innocent men and women, sometimes for no other reason than having the wrong last names? And how did the citizenry finally take back the county from those warring incessantly against each other?

Left: Present-day Rowan County remains largely agricultural. *Public domain.*

Below: The armed Hatfields of the infamous Hatfield-McCoy feud. *Courtesy of the Kentucky Historical Society.*

Fortunately, the "troubles," as some called it, have been chronicled in many books, articles and scholarly journals that look at the feud from several different angles in attempts to analyze its causes and understand the factors that would bring such a dark period to the emerald hills of eastern Kentucky. Most notable are Fred Brown Jr. and Juanita Blair's *Days of Anger, Days of Tears*, John Ed Pearce's *Days of Darkness* and the work of anthropologist Keith F. Otterbein at the University of Buffalo. These various sources, as well as looking back through the more objective lens of history, have allowed us to answer some of the more obvious questions regarding the era.

WHY SO MANY FEUDS?

Many from other parts of the Commonwealth wonder why so many of these feuds occurred in the most mountainous part of the state. The answer seems to be that the often-maligned people who eventually settled that part of Kentucky were either Scots-Irish or people from the borderlands between southern Scotland and Northern England. The Borderlanders especially had endured a long history of feuds going back, according to Keith Otterbein, to before the Norman Conquest in 1066.

The feuds in the United Kingdom reached their heights during the reign of James I of England in and around the time of Shakespeare, when the residents of the area had gathered into tight-knit clans, often composed of family members, their children and the in-laws of that family. Each of the families was headed by a revered or at least deeply respected patriarch whose influence on the younger members was considerable, a factor quite obvious in the feuds in the Commonwealth as well.

Typically, the feuds in the British Isles had to do with cattle rustling—one clan stealing another clan's source of income and food, causing the first group to seek some sort of retaliation. The feuds in Kentucky also had a commercial emphasis to them, although the commodity didn't have four legs but rather usually came in liquid form in a barrel with a plug in it.

When the Borderlanders immigrated to the United States, they were soon met by the same sort of prejudice they had endured back home—only this time it was the East Coast of the United States, forcing them to push farther westward into the largely unsettled mountains of Kentucky, Tennessee and surrounding areas. Many others acquired land in the same area as payment for service in the Revolutionary War.

Yet the British ancestors also bequeathed another important part of feuds near or far: a keen sense of honor. Because of their geographic isolation and their emphasis on individualism as small-time farmers and herders back in the British Isles, the Borderlanders developed a clear and clinging sense of what honor meant and how it should be shown.

Before the Civil War, southerners in most parts of the South, including the uplands, had a similar sense of honor and respect. Some would argue that southerners even today show more overt signs and gestures of respect than their more reticent neighbors in the North.

Otterbein and others who study the causes of feuds also often cite the aftermath of the Civil War as the roiling breeding grounds for the many murderous feuds of Kentucky, with the ex-Union men coming back as Republicans and the ex-Rebels returning as devoted Democrats.

While the sympathies of the mountaineers are most often characterized as strictly pro-Union, that generalization did not always hold. In fact, while there was little slavery throughout the region and strong Northern sentiment in spots, many mountain residents showed strong Southern sentiment, with numerous folk stubbornly committed to the South because they sincerely believed that the Confederacy was less likely to interfere in their everyday life. After all, they just wanted to be left alone. However, there were some mountaineers who were so independent that their sympathies swayed with the circumstances.

But generally speaking, after the war, weary veterans from both sides returned to what had to be a hostile environment where your neighbor had fought on the opposite side of the war. In other words, at one time, that same neighbor may have wanted to kill you, hardly making for hospitable relations. Add to that, as one authority says, the fact that both sides came back to the mountains with a rather sophisticated knowledge of new and more powerful weapons. The firearms were no longer just the muzzle-loaded squirrel guns, accurate at only a few yards, that many marched off to war with; now the former soldiers possessed the more sophisticated Colt revolvers and Winchester rifles designed to kill at greater distances and with considerably more accuracy—guns just right for ambushes, battles and gun fights of all kinds.

With such seething anger and resentment spreading like a morning fog in the mountains and valleys, with a long history of feuding dating back to the mother country and with veterans of war still with scores to settle with neighbors who, like them, carried more powerful arms, it was not surprising that hostility would break out in the mountains in several places—as it most certainly did.

The tiny spark that lit the flame of riotous murder and mayhem of the feuds in the region didn't really have to be that important. It could be accusations of stealing horses or livestock—hogs, for example, in the Hatfield-McCoy feud. It could be a raucous, eye-gouging fistfight energized by too much raw whiskey or maybe some thoughtless insult to a party's honor or dignity. What mattered most was that the circumstances—in the eyes of the participants, at least—demanded some kind of violent response, usually some kind of revenge killing.

But as Otterbein points out, the killings did not necessarily end up in a tit-for-tat sequence. More people on one side, for instance, could be killed than on the other.

THE BEGINNINGS OF THE ROWAN COUNTY WARS: THE MARTINS AND TOLLIVERS

In the Rowan County War, it all began rather innocently in the intense environment of postwar Morehead, the county seat of Rowan County, where tension was stretched as taut as electric wires, impatient for something to shock the nervous parties into action.

It all began as a simple mistake.

At a dance in Morehead in 1883, William Trumbo's wife, Lucy, weary from the evening, decided to retire to her hotel room to relax, away from the music and festivities downstairs. But somehow, she mistakenly managed to go not to her room but the room of a wealthy businessman named H.G. Price. Later, when Price went to his room, he found Mrs. Trumbo lying on his bed, extending what he took to be an obvious invitation. Screaming and showing all measures of protest, Mrs. Martin leapt from the room, rushed downstairs and told her distraught husband about her rather innocent conduct and the boorish behavior of Price.

While what transpired would ordinarily be laughed off by both parties, one fact prevented the incident from being soon forgotten: Lucy was related by birth and marriage to two prominent and powerful Republican families in Rowan County—the Martins and the Logans—and they saw nothing particularly funny about Lucy Trumbo's episode in Price's hotel room.

Later, on election day (already an occasion for vote buying, fisticuffs and general bad behavior), Trumbo confronted Price and in no certain terms demanded a full apology—something that Price was unwilling to give, considering the circumstances.

Soon, words turned to fists and an all-out brawl broke out, resulting in a father of seven, Solomon Bradley, a Martin man, stumbling dead to the floor, the victim of a gunshot.

Amid all the chaos, Floyd Tolliver, an ardent Democrat and no friend of the Martins, and John Martin began a tussle that climaxed with both men drawing arms and Martin being wounded. All the madness resulted in indictments for both Tolliver and Martin, since nobody was quite sure who shot poor Mr. Bradley.

While awaiting trial, John Martin and Floyd Tolliver met again at a Morehead hotel when both had enough whiskey in them to lose their sense of danger. Angry words and loud recriminations soon flew between them, and John Martin outdrew Floyd Tolliver, sending Tolliver stumbling to the floor, uttering the ominous dying words to his sympathizers, "Remember what you swore to do. You said you'd kill him. Keep your word."

Floyd Tolliver's brother, Craig, swore to uphold the family honor and to comply with his late brother's final wishes, accusations that prompted the authorities to transfer John Martin to a jail in Clark County, far enough away and safe enough to keep Craig Tolliver from reaping his revenge.

Or so they thought.

Craig Tolliver had a plan. He or someone in his gang would write a request to the unaware jailer in Clark County to turn over Martin to the Tolliver gang, forge the signature of an appropriate Rowan County official, secure the release of the hapless Martin and murder him on the train back to Morehead.

Despite the vigorous protests of Martin himself, the Clark County jailer complied with what he thought was a legitimate transfer of a prisoner. As the train reached the community of Farmers, the home of the Tollivers, Martin, shackled and cuffed, was grabbed from his train car and promptly riddled with bullets from a gang of revenge-minded Tollivers. Shortly thereafter, the deputy sheriff, a Martin protégé, was also gunned down while riding by Christy Creek, out in the county.

The Martin side would hardly just put their hands in their pockets and shake their heads. Rowan County sheriff Cook Humphrey, a Martin sympathizer, confronted the Tolliver men on the streets of Morehead, now virtually in the hands of Craig Tolliver and his minions. Soon, words were no longer adequate and a fierce battle broke out on the Morehead streets, with guns ablaze and havoc in charge, while frightened residents scrambled to safety and ducked for cover.

RESIDENTS SEEK HELP

The fray so alarmed the townspeople that some caught a train to Frankfort to appeal to Governor J. Proctor Knott for some kind of help. Governor Knott sent Adjutant General John Castleman to Morehead to broker some kind of peace. Duly summoned, the warring parties met in Louisville and on April 11, 1885, agreed to cease and desist from any kind of armed warfare and vowed to live together peacefully. In exchange for promises from both the Martin and Tolliver sides to end the feud, both parties would have all charges against them dismissed.

But promises were cheap, and neither side had any serious notions about living up to the terms of the agreement.

Soon, a rumor made its way to Morehead, where Craig Tolliver was ensconced as town marshal, that Sheriff Cook Humphrey and John Martin had devised an elaborate plan to take the county tax money and flee west.

Craig Tolliver wasn't going to miss this opportunity, so he and a gang of supporters rode out to the home of Dr. Ben Martin after hearing that Humphrey was holed up there. Dr. Martin, fearing for his life, had already fled the violence and left his wife and children back in Rowan County while he made housing arrangements elsewhere.

Soon, the Martin house was surrounded, bullets flying through windowpanes and pandemonium reigning. In the shootout, Craig Tolliver suffered a shotgun blast to the face while trying to sneak into the Martin house. But the siege didn't bring out Humphrey, who had escaped to the hills, and the wounded but still alive Craig Tolliver, out of frustration more than strategy, set the Martin home ablaze, its flames licking the night sky and soothing his pent-up anger.

The following day, troops under the command of Major Lewis McKee arrived in Morehead, bent on restoring order. But they failed to get many indictments in the courts, and most parties, guilty and otherwise, were freed. While the soldiers were there, peace came to the mountain hamlet. But perhaps feeling the lull in violence was only temporary, many Morehead residents used this time to scamper away, seeking tranquility in neighboring counties and even in faraway places like Kansas and Iowa.

When the militia left on August 8, the seething embers of anger burst into flames again, resulting in yet another gun battle in Morehead and another visit from the state militia. This time, the government called in Commonwealth Attorney Asher Caruth, who got Humphrey and Tolliver to sign an agreement that dropped all charges against them but stipulated that both were to leave Morehead permanently.

Both signed, Humphrey left town and Tolliver absented himself from Morehead just long enough to get all charges dropped so that when he returned, he was elected to county judge. With a Tolliver supporter as town marshal, Craig Tolliver had a stranglehold on Rowan County, something the citizenry was reminded of with the frequent displays of celebratory gunfire.

After still more killings to eliminate still more Tolliver enemies—punctuated by the senseless slaughter of two Logan brothers falsely charged with conspiring to murder a Tolliver ally—Daniel Boone Logan had finally had his fill. After organizing a group of supporters, Logan set out for

Frankfort, where he met with Governor Knott, who by this time probably wondered what he could possibly do to bring Rowan County to its senses. The governor barked at Logan, "You're going to have to settle your own affairs," a remark that Logan took to heart.

On cue, Logan was off to Cincinnati, where he purchased a large assortment of Winchester rifles and other assorted weapons of war. When he arrived back in Morehead, he had over one hundred men patiently waiting for the rare opportunity to rid the county of the Tollivers.

On June 22, with the town surrounded, Logan and his men called Craig Tolliver out of one of his many businesses. And soon, from behind bushes, corners, lumberyards and wherever men with guns could hide, a two-hour battle raged on, dealing death and destruction to Tollivers. Before dying, Craig ceremoniously removed his boots, having vowed earlier never to die with his boots on.

THE AFTERMATH OF THE FEUD

The rule of the terrible Tollivers was over. But there was still much work to do if the county wanted to put itself back together, so newly elected governor Simon Bolivar Buckner commissioned an extensive report from a committee headed by General Sam Hill to study conditions in the county and to recommend courses of action.

General Hill's report of November 22, 1887, consisted of a series of stinging accusations about the causes of the deadly feud and the catalytic conditions that kept the flames from dying. He singled out what he called "the want of more sentiment in the county." He detailed the domineering "criminal element" in charge of the county. He criticized the county's apparent "warmest sympathy with crime and criminals." He even lambasted the grand jury that appeared designed to "shield the strong and guilty and punish the weak and helpless."

It was hardly a flattering picture, but Rowan County residents seemed to take it to heart, and soon the lush green hills and narrow valleys that had echoed gunfire were again quiet while memories faded of a time when Rowan County seemed to be at war with itself.

Chapter 6
Kentucky Goes to War: Saltpeter Works at Mammoth Cave

Although Native Americans used the cavern as long ago as 4000 BC, in the late eighteenth century, legend has it that the first European American to find Mammoth Cave was John Houchins, who, so the story goes, was chasing a wounded bear at the time of his discovery.

Whether or not it was Houchins, chances are that the first frontiersman to enter the cave wouldn't have been thinking only of a bearskin rug or greasy bear meat; one of the questions on the minds of most early explorers and settlers stepping into the cave would have been, "Would this be a good source of saltpeter?" In fact, one of the popular *Foxfire* books says that "one of the principle objectives of exploring new territory was to find saltpeter caves."

While saltpeter (or potassium nitrate, its chemical name) has a number of uses as a preservative or medicine, its main function in frontier days was as the chief ingredient in gunpowder, called black powder today. At this point in the history of explosives, black powder was the only gunpowder available.

Of course, gunpowder was vastly important to the early pioneers since it was the power behind the flintlock rifles that provided meat for the table and protection against marauding Native Americans, carnivorous animals and other enemies. And because these early settlers lived many miles from the nearest supply store, they had to make their own gunpowder—as they did in practically every other facet of frontier life.

While saltpeter can be made in a number of different ways, properly processed cave sediment produces some of the richest sources, and Mammoth Cave saltpeter was considered by many to be the best of the best.

THE WAR OF 1812 SPARKS A SALTPETER BOOM

Aside from the outstanding quality of the saltpeter extracted from Mammoth Cave, there's much more to the story of saltpeter processing in the largest cave system in the world (more than 350 miles explored so far, a figure growing each year as brave spelunkers push farther and farther into the limestone labyrinth).

It should not be surprising, then, that when word spread about Mammoth Cave's enormous potential for saltpeter production, investors would soon follow. This would not be a small-time operation; it would need serious investors. And these investors appeared in the form of two Kentuckians: Fleming Gatewood, who was from the immediate area, and Charles Wilkins, a saltpeter buyer from Lexington. Although Gatewood later sold his interest to Hyman Gratz, by 1810, according to historians Carol A. Hill and Duane DePaepe, large-scale saltpeter mining had gotten under way in Mammoth Cave, with Archibald Miller managing the operation.

Yet there was a clear sense of immediacy about the production of saltpeter at this time in the nation's history. As the result of a number of embargo acts passed during the Thomas Jefferson administration and imposed on trade mainly with Great Britain, the usual source of gunpowder through the British Isles from India was rapidly drying up for those living on the east coast of the new republic.

England had, to a degree, been stingy with the sale of gunpowder to Americans, fearing before the Revolutionary War that the colonists would use the gunpowder on British troops stationed in what were then the colonies. Americans, however, needed more gunpowder.

But two British policies enacted a few years after the Revolutionary War itself seriously strained relations with the United States. First, the British navy had willfully impressed American sailors on American ships, presumably looking for deserters from the British navy. At the time, England was at war with Napoleon Bonaparte and France, but the policy of shanghaiing American sailors attacked the fragile dignity and sovereignty of the young nation. In fact, many of those same men were eventually forced into service on British ships. In addition, the British, fearing that the United States was supplying France with war materials, seriously sought to limit U.S. trade with anyone but England, another insult to the pride of young America.

Stretching back to 1807, the embargo acts, even though self-imposed in hopes of forcing the reform of England's trade policies, also significantly affected many phases of the American economy by forcing the young country to rely more on their own resources rather than foreign products. During those years leading up to a second war with England, eventually declared on June 18, 1812, the price of saltpeter soared, making its production a highly profitable venture.

When entrepreneurs Gatewood and Flatt first gazed into Mammoth Cave, aided by lamps lit by lard, they must have felt they had the perfect place for their operation. First, they noticed the steady and ample drip of water at the very entrance of the cave, which meant that the water necessary in the leaching process would not have to be lugged from a source far away. Then, upon entering, they found an enormous room with a high ceiling in which to set up the equipment the production of saltpeter demanded. Today called the Rotunda, the area features not only a constant room temperature in the mid-fifties but also a generous supply of cave sediment on the floor of the cave. While bat guano can be processed into saltpeter, even richer ore is the calcium nitrate present in the settlings on this cave's floor, washed there in the water that formed the cave millions of years ago.

And as Gatewood and Flatt found their way back farther, the cave opened up to still another room suitable for additional equipment, dubbed Booth's Amphitheater, with the added promise of seemingly endless passages that could also be mined.

Finally, they must have noticed that the sediment on the cave's floor was especially rich. According to *Foxfire 5*, the common test for the richness of the cave dirt was to make a footprint in it and come back twenty-four hours later. If the print was barely visible, the sediment was considered a rich source for making saltpeter, and Mammoth Cave certainly passed that test.

All these factors made Mammoth Cave an ideal place for the production of saltpeter in a burgeoning market. Especially interested in Mammoth Cave's quality saltpeter was E.I. DuPont, who had fled France to avoid religious persecution and had begun manufacturing gunpowder in Wilmington, Delaware, where he further purified the saltpeter and mixed it with appropriate amounts of charcoal and sulphur to complete the process.

MAKING SALTPETER IN MAMMOTH CAVE

As Hill and DePaepe note, making saltpeter with cave dirt was a fairly simple chemical operation. First, the slaves, as many as seventy of them, broke up the cave sediment down to a depth of about twenty-four to thirty-six inches

A vat used in gathering cave dust for making saltpeter in Mammoth Cave. *Author's collection.*

using a mattock and then filled gunny sacks with the sediment. These sacks were then transported by ox cart to the square leaching vats. Cave historian Burton Faust says that the box-shaped vats were 12 feet wide, 13 feet long and 3 feet deep, holding about 460 cubic feet of dirt. Later vats were v-shaped, apparently to make them easier to assemble and disassemble.

Next, the workers continuously poured water over the sediment in order to leach out the nitrates present. They then drained that liquid from the straw-lined vats and allowed the mixture, now called either "mother liquor" or "beer," to sit for twenty-four hours. For this first part of the operation, the water was piped by gravity into the leaching vat area from the mouth of the cave through an elaborate series of wooden pipes. According to Faust, these pipes were made from straight logs, measuring about six to nine inches around and up to twenty-six feet in length, that had been augered to form a straight, sturdy and hollow pipe. After that, the logs were beveled on each end in opposite directions so that they would fit snugly together with another similarly formed pipe.

In the next stage in the process, the mother liquor that had collected in the vats had to be piped out of the cave by means of crude hand-operated pumps. Because there were two places of operation, the Rotunda and Booth's Amphitheatre, pumps were placed on fifteen-foot-tall rock towers near each location. An additional pump was situated at the cave's entrance to enhance the flow of the leached liquid out of the cave.

Once outside of the cave, the solution had to be converted from calcium nitrate to potassium nitrate, or saltpeter. To do that, workers combined the mother liquor with potash in the form of charcoal made, according to Faust, from hardwoods such as oak, hickory and chestnut. Adding the charcoal produced a white substance known as "curds," which fell to the bottom of a large kettle. More and more wood ashes were added until the solution no longer yielded curds.

The solution was now ready for the next phase of the process, which involved boiling the liquid in what Faust calls "boiling furnaces" or enormous copper kettles, as large as five hundred gallons at some saltpeter operations. Added to the solution during the boiling, according to Faust and *Foxfire 5*, were two rather odd ingredients: turnip halves, to keep the solution from foaming, and ox blood, which caused the foreign substances to rise to the top, where workers continually skimmed it off.

After the solution was boiled for a few hours, it was allowed to cool. As it cooled, the solution formed what one source calls "fine, bitter, needle-shaped crystals of potassium nitrate" or saltpeter, which was then dried, gathered by a worker, placed in bags and transported to another location, where it was converted into gunpowder.

For saltpeter processed at Mammoth Cave, that place would have been the DuPont Powder Works plant in Wilmington, Delaware. It's easy to understand that as the War of 1812 heated up, DuPont demanded more and more saltpeter from Mammoth Cave. But something that happened on December 16, 1811, and on several other occasions seriously interrupted the production of saltpeter in the cave—an event, in fact, hundreds of miles away.

AN EARTHQUAKE RUMBLES THROUGH MAMMOTH CAVE

On December 16, 1811, near the westernmost part of Kentucky, in a little Missouri town on the Mississippi River called New Madrid, the earth began to rumble, roll and shake in the throes of the strongest earthquake ever to hit the forty-eight contiguous states, stronger than even the San Francisco earthquake that turned that city to rubble in 1906.

One shock would have been enough, but major aftershocks shook the earth on January 23, 1812, and again on February 7. In fact, by the time the earth settled down again, hundreds of aftershocks occurred for about a year, with major shocks felt as far away as Boston and Washington, D.C. Had the region closest to the epicenter been as populated as it is today, the damage and loss of life would be almost incalculable.

And, of course, the earthquake and its aftermath was felt in Mammoth Cave, too, where laborers were busy at work. But until Angelo I. George and Gary O'Dell explored the subject in a January 1992 article, nobody really understood the full magnitude of the effects of the earthquake and aftershocks on saltpeter mining in the cave.

By 1812, Mammoth Cave's saltpeter production had inexplicably come to a virtual halt. Many other historians have tried to explain why Mammoth Cave wasn't producing its usual excellent quality of saltpeter, but George and O'Dell discovered a previously unknown letter from Archibald McCall, a purchasing agent for DuPont in Philadelphia, to E.I. DuPont that details the many repairs that had to be done as a result of the earthquake damage to the equipment in the cave. One problem, for example, was that one of the pump towers "sank three feet in the ground," something that suddenly made the gravity flow of water into the cave unworkable.

Did the floor of the cave actually sink that much?

George and O'Dell argue that the cave floor didn't really sink. As they noted, the pump towers rested not on the cave floor but rather on waste cave sediment that built up as earlier workers discarded the waste dirt that had already been leached for its minerals. With the area around the vats continuously wet, the stones in the pump tower naturally sank into the waste material when the earthquake hit. Problems like this, as well as many others, had to be solved before the saltpeter operation could resume.

But there was also psychological damage, as both managers and workers refused to enter the cave, fearing for their lives. Add to that the discovery of an ancient mummy of a Native American, named Fawn Hoof, found in nearby Short Cave and then placed in Mammoth Cave in a region called Haunted Chambers and the appearance of the Great Comet of 1812, and many workers started to believe that the cave was the "passage to Hell itself."

By late 1813, the saltpeter mining in Mammoth Cave had ceased, and DuPont shortly suspended his contract with the mining company. By 1815, the War of 1812 had ended, and the price of saltpeter had gone down so dramatically that any operation in the cave had been discontinued. Yet much of the equipment still lies on the floor of the cave, preserved for nearly two hundred years by the cave's unique atmosphere.

In his book on Kentucky in the War of 1812, Anderson Chenault Quisenberry estimates that over 83 percent of the available men in Kentucky volunteered for the war effort. And along with the saltpeter works at Mammoth Cave, those men helped maintain the sovereign rights of the young democracy.

On the battlefield and in Mammoth Cave, Kentucky once again was up to the challenge.

Chapter 7
Nails, Kettles and Plows:
A Brief History of Iron Smelting in Early Kentucky

Scattered all along the highways of Kentucky are interesting state historical markers. Some of the metal signs mark the birthplace or home of famous Kentuckians, like Joseph Holt in Breckinridge County or Andrew Jackson Smith in Lyon County. Some, like those at Wildcat Mountain and Middle Creek, describe the spot where some significant event took place, such as a battle or skirmish during the Civil War. And some even describe unusual natural settings, like the world's tallest sassafras tree in Owensboro or Natural Bridge in Slade.

The inquisitive often find themselves pulling off the side of the road, rolling their windows down and craning their necks to read what the signs have to offer. The signs help us to understand our state's history, to appreciate what those who came before us had to endure and to better understand the rich culture and diversity of the Commonwealth.

SMELTING ACROSS THE STATE

What is fascinating about many of these markers is that nearly seventy of them refer to iron smelting furnaces that once squatted on hillsides all over the state. These furnaces were located in not only the forested areas of the eastern Kentucky mountains but also in the middle part of the state and even in the far western reaches of the Commonwealth. The historical markers spell out a smelting industry that, in the 1830s, made Kentucky the third-leading producer of iron in the entire country.

The remains of an iron-making furnace in Estill County. *Author's collection.*

According to the Kentucky Geological Survey, iron ore, albeit hardly of the highest grade, exists in several counties in the state. The "most significant iron ore deposits" are found in Bath and Menifee Counties, with reserves of "several million tons."

Deposits of a different geological composition were mined in Boyd, Carter and Greenup Counties, a part of the "Hanging Rock Iron Region," which also stretched into parts of southern Ohio.

Caldwell, Trigg and Lyon Counties smelted iron, too, but the presence of iron ore in its many forms was so meager that iron smelting proved to be "not economical." Other counties also had iron furnaces, like those in Bullitt and Estill Counties, with still others scattered in various pockets all across the state wherever iron ore was of the quality to be economically and efficiently smelted.

Normally, most people don't think of the Commonwealth as a source of iron ore like they do the Great Lakes region, particularly the Mesabi Range and the rest of the massive Iron Range in northeastern Minnesota. That area became the source of iron ore for smelting in the mills of Pittsburgh, Pennsylvania; Middletown, Ohio; and Birmingham, Alabama, and turned out high-grade steel, the metal skeletons of massive buildings that rise proudly from the soils of American cities.

Yet as fledgling Americans pushed west from the coastal cities of the eastern seaboard, they moved farther from things they needed, like nails to build buildings, iron pots to produce salt, cooking pots, plowshares, skillets and flat irons, just to name a few. Of course, they needed steel for guns and axes, but the Bessemer method of producing steel efficiently and cheaply lay many years in the future.

While those products could be shipped to eager customers on the frontier, the roads were often mere paths, old buffalo trails or dried creek beds, making shipping goods over the mountains a daunting task for any merchant who wished to sell his wares. Besides, at that time, there weren't enough customers to justify the enormous shipping costs incurred by merchants and middlemen from the east coast of colonial America.

THE NEED FOR AND THE PRODUCTION OF IRON ON THE FRONTIER

But the early settlers of the Commonwealth were far from helpless. Largely self-sustaining, they grew or raised their own food, rendered fat to make soap, planted flax to make their own linen, spun their own wool, built their cabins and homes out of the wood and stone that surrounded them, obtained their own sweetening from sorghum, rendered lard for cooking and distilled their unique brand of spirits for social and medicinal purposes. If they needed gunpowder, they found a nearby cave and mined it for the minerals necessary to make their own explosives. If they needed salt, they found a salt lick and boiled the saline solution until they had the commodity so necessary to sustain life in the far-reaching frontier.

Often, though, the early residents needed products that could be made only of iron.

To produce iron in its various forms, smelters required several things found in early Kentucky: charcoal, iron ore, some sort of power and a cadre of men, trained and untrained, to do the dirty, sweaty and often confining jobs of keeping the furnaces hot and the metal flowing. While gentlemen of wealth often financed the construction of furnaces, iron making was hardly a gentleman's job.

The lush virgin forests of Kentucky proved to be a ready source of wood to make charcoal. An integral part of the iron smelting operation required a crew of men whose only job was to turn Kentucky hardwoods and softwoods into charcoal, a necessary element in order to raise the temperature of the iron ore to a melting point. Therefore, it's not really surprising that the center of iron smelting in the state was amidst the dense forests of the Appalachian Mountains.

In *Old Kentucky Iron Furnaces*, noted Kentucky historian J. Winston Coleman says that sometimes a crew of eight to ten men, called colliers, were necessary to keep one furnace supplied with enough charcoal, a process that took three to ten days to complete. In the latter part of the nineteenth century, coal replaced charcoal as the fuel of choice, but coal mining soon proved to be more profitable than iron smelting itself as the riches of the eastern and western Kentucky coal fields were discovered and mined.

Another group of men had the responsibility of mining the ore itself. The ore, of course, was not the only solid rock necessary for iron smelting, for some sort of flux, usually limestone, was necessary to coax out the iron from the ore. This meant that those providing the raw materials were responsible for both the ore itself and some sort of agent necessary for the conversion of the ore to iron. The men dug, blasted and broke up the raw materials and loaded and transported them into the furnace. Sometimes, the work was done by slaves, but regardless of whomever did the backbreaking work, the task was nothing less than tiresome and exhausting.

The furnace to be filled was relatively simple in design, with a broad base at the bottom, called the hearth. Coleman notes that, like the rest of the furnace, this part was made of sandstone and was about twenty-five feet wide. From there, the furnace neck narrowed sharply until it reached a height that varied considerably but was anywhere from twenty-five to forty feet, forming the chimney of the furnace.

To ease the loading procedure, Coleman says that the furnace often rested on the side of a hill, with a narrow path etched out of the hill above the stack to provide easy access for the loading of charcoal, limestone flux and the ore itself. Since the furnace could not draw enough oxygen by itself to melt the ore, some sort of system for providing sharp streams of air was necessary to get the ore hot enough to actually produce a flow of iron. These devices, called bellows, were usually driven by the force of a nearby stream and raised the temperature inside the furnace enough so that melted iron flowed out of the bottom of the furnace.

In the iron production process, when the conditions were right and the fire in the middle of the furnace was hot enough, the charcoal mixed with the excess oxygen in the ore itself, partially separating the iron from the other members of the mixture. One element, the crushed limestone, provided a flux for the mixture; that is, when burned, it actually helped rid the molten iron of impurities. This produced a melted mixture of impurities and iron, with the impurities, called slag, floating on top of the heavier iron from the foot of the furnace. The slag was then diverted away from the iron as the hot metal followed a path into a long, carefully arranged series of trenches made of sand and some clay. The trenches were laid out so that one large trench was positioned perpendicular to several shorter trenches. The system was said to look like a sow nursing her pigs, with the sow being the larger trench and the short trenches resembling her pigs. When cooled, the product was thus called "pig iron," and it was now ready for further refining and to be cast into various iron products like iron kettles or nails. Pig iron itself is too brittle and not useful for much else other than further refining to turn it into wrought iron or steel.

THE FITCHBURG FURNACE

These iron-smelting furnaces often became the center of an entire community, called an "iron plantation." The operation at Fitchburg in Estill County serves as a good example.

According to the *Lexington Herald-Leader*, the elaborate furnace at Fitchburg was actually two furnaces built together as one structure, with two steam engines acting as bellows. Financed by a large group of New England investors, headed by Frank and Fred Fitch, the furnace became the focus of life in a community called Fitchburg, named for the two brothers. Built in 1868–69, the community of workers and their families soon swelled to a village of nearly two thousand people, composed of both natives and immigrants from various European countries. Employees cut the trees to make the charcoal, mined the ore nearby and operated the furnace while a crew managed a tram to tow the pig iron to the Kentucky River for shipping—all were necessary parts of an elaborate industry dependent upon iron smelting. Surrounding the furnace were ornate mansions for the financiers, while bungalows, various stores, a church and a school dotted the landscape. In 1873, a national economic panic eventually closed the plant forever, leaving the now out-of-work Fitchburg residents to find other work someplace else.

In 2004, the citizens of Estill County organized a group called Friends of the Fitchburg Furnace. After receiving a government grant of $670,000 that year, the Fitchburg Furnace has been largely restored to its original condition and opened to the public. Members of the committee, like Robert "Skip" Johnson, have planned to record the furnace's history in book form, containing an older history of the furnace, along with a master's project devoted to Fitchburg by David Patrick Thompson at the University of Kentucky.

While the Fitchburg of the late 1860s and early 1870s is no longer there, visitors can still get a good idea of how iron smelting took place in nineteenth-century America as they envision the remnants of an industry once the center of a bustling community.

Like many of the iron furnaces themselves, the heavy forests surrounding them soon rapidly disappeared as more and more charcoal was needed and there were fewer and fewer trees to fill that need. Besides depleting the wood supply available, much of the iron ore in Kentucky was, according to geologist Dr. Tom Lierman, "extremely impure and contaminated with silicon dioxide (quartz)"compared to the rich ore in the Wisconsin and Minnesota Iron Range.

Iron smelting evolved out of the early settlers' need for iron and iron-based products. The industry is a vivid testimony not only to their backbreaking

Blacksmiths often crafted tools and utensils out of pig iron. *Public domain.*

work but also their deep commitment to making the most of the rich resources of the state.

Yet in many ways, we have lost our understanding of just how vast iron smelting was in the state. Many of the old iron furnaces are now covered with weeds and vines, their stones crumbling from age and neglect, and hidden from public view.

My thanks to Dr. Tom Lierman of Eastern Kentucky University and Robert "Skip" Johnson for their expertise.

Chapter 8

Henry Clay:
Great Kentucky Senator,
Great Friend of Horses

In 1955, during his service in the U.S. Senate, President John F. Kennedy chaired a committee to select the five most outstanding senators in the country's history. While the committee struggled to agree on all five, Henry Clay of Kentucky was an easy choice.

Known as the "Great Compromiser," Clay's memorable oratory and skilled diplomacy probably had much to do with delaying the Civil War by decades. In fact, one of Clay's colleagues said that there would have been no Civil War if Henry Clay had been alive.

Yet while most people know that Clay unsuccessfully ran for the presidency several times, few know that the golden-throated orator made a significant contribution to the horse industry in the Bluegrass State. In an age that depended little on machinery to do agricultural work, Clay began producing stout and tireless mules, animals so valuable to the farms and plantations of Old Kentucky and elsewhere in the South. Securing breeding stock from as far away as France and Spain, Clay sought to meet the demand by breeding some of the finest mules in the country on his Ashland plantation, six hundred sprawling acres of land just outside Lexington.

Yet like the gentlemen farmers of his native Virginia, Clay soon experimented with horseflesh. While the Old Dominion was home to a variety of breeds of horses and, in fact, a leader in that industry, these elegant breeds were soon transplanted to Kentucky soil as more and more Virginians moved west.

A portrait of Kentucky senator Henry Clay, a highly influential politician and horse breeder. *Courtesy of the Kentucky Historical Society.*

KENTUCKIANS LOVE HORSES

Along with the horses themselves, the pioneers of Kentucky brought with them a deep and abiding devotion to the animals. They loved all manner of horses from racing steeds to work horses. And according to the authors of *Horse World*, of all of the folkways and attitudes that crossed the Cumberland Mountains, none "was more entrenched than an admiration for fine domestic animals and a pastoral economy." The product of a middle-class

Virginia family, Clay would have understood the prevailing attitudes of his fellow Kentucky transplants.

The rolling bluegrass, waving in gentle and wispy breezes and flourishing in the mild climate and limestone-leeched loam, provided a rich source of feed for these elegant animals. In *Horse World*, the authors are even more specific about why the Bluegrass Region is so well suited to raising strong, resilient horses. They note that the rich soil contains a "remarkable content of calcium phosphate and small quantities of trace elements needed by animals." The same source also points out that the region's water comes mainly from springs that absorbed some of those essential minerals. In the end, the soil and water "aid in the formation of solid but light bones, strong tendons, strong firm and elastic muscles, and favor general stamina."

CLAY BEGINS BREEDING HORSES

Apparently aware of the unique qualities that the Bluegrass Region presented for the development of race horses, Clay soon began breeding more and more racing steeds, something that prompted him to build his own racetrack at Ashland. This was a luxury he could afford, according to one of his biographers, Robert Remini, because his "superior breeds" won so many races and accumulated so much money.

Ashland, the home of Senator Henry Clay, was located on his large farm near Lexington. *Courtesy of the Kentucky Historical Society.*

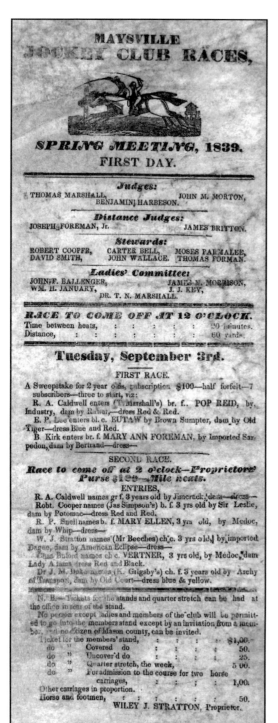

But fast horses don't come from mediocre ancestors, so Clay began buying expensive horseflesh. First came Turf Horse Buzzard, a steed purchased by Clay and four other men in 1808 for a whopping $5,500, a gigantic outlay of cash for the day. Jeff Meyer, an expert on the Clay family's contribution to the horse industry, records that while Buzzard was a quality horse, he had only a single eye and a bad hip and lived only two more years, but the stud became "a prominent sire."

Indeed, the steady progress in many areas of agriculture at Ashland prompted Clay to remark, "I am getting a passion for rural occupations." In a letter to a friend, Clay confided that maybe he ought to give up politics altogether, concluding, "I shall not be unhappy if a sense of public duty shall leave me free to pursue my

An early advertisement for a horseracing meet. Courtesy of the Kentucky Historical Society.

present inclinations." Later, he modestly admitted that he would "make a better farmer than a statesman." In fact, one biographer concludes that Clay always thought of himself as a farmer and that politics and law were merely sidelines that provided the money needed to purchase the land and animals that boarded at Ashland.

And surely Clay loved the life of a farmer and the ability to augment his income by breeding fine horses and experimenting with imported Hereford and Durham cattle, various kinds of sheep and pigs and crops like corn and hemp. Yet when he was away, his papers and letters are filled with references to his horses, detailing directions for the careful husbandry of his animals. In one letter to his son, Henry Jr., the elder Clay is quite specific about what he wanted: "Tell Mr. [William] Martin that I wish the Wickliffe mare put to Stamboul, the Arabian mare to Shakespeare, and the Virginia mare to my neighbor Mr. Hunt's horse." In addition, archival records reveal that Clay kept extensive accounts on the breeding records for many of his animals, including horses.

As Meyer notes, Clay, an inveterate gambler (especially at poker and whist), began racing for money as early as 1809, when he entered a race with a $300 purse between two descendants of Spread Eagle, a race Clay lost. He also became a member of the Lexington Jockey Club, an organization that symbolized the rapid rise of and enduring interest in the horse industry in the Bluegrass State.

CLAY SETTLES ON THOROUGHBREDS

By the early 1830s, Clay ceased his dabbling in all other breeds of horses and concentrated almost exclusively on thoroughbreds. That same year, he mirrored that interest by founding what he called the Ashland Thoroughbred Stock Farm in an attempt to commit himself to breeding thoroughbreds.

Perhaps the racing fever steered him in this direction, so when the Sultan Mohamoud presented four beautiful Arabian horses to a diplomat in Constantinople and the U.S. government nixed the presents as unconstitutional, Clay quickly bought half interest in steeds called Stamboul and Kocklani.

In 1835, he acquired a brood mare, Allegrante, originally the property of Virginia governor James Barbour, for $1,500. The governor told him that Allegrante was "the finest filly you have seen."

But the Clay who didn't like to mix politics with agriculture soon found out that one could be the benefactor of the other. In 1845, after a visit to South Carolinian Colonel Wade Hampton, Clay found a horse called Margaret Wood already at Ashland, a gift given to Clay by this generous Southerner because of the high esteem he held for the "Great Compromiser." Meyer notes that Margaret Wood soon proved her worth by winning the Trial Stakes in Nashville and later giving birth to a foal named Heraldry, a successful winner in her own right as well as a prominent broodmare in the Ashland stables.

According to Joseph Rogers, another Clay biographer, one of Margaret Woods's offspring, a horse called Wade Hampton, wasn't blessed with both speed and sense but rather something Rogers calls "a villainous disposition." On occasion, he seemed to enjoy racing and consistently won big. Yet on other occasions, he seemed to be totally unmanageable and bucked even the gentlest jockey out of the saddle.

In New Orleans, for instance, Wade Hampton seemed primed and pumped for the big race, prompting several wealthy backers to bet on his fortune. He got off well out of the starting gate, quickly taking the lead, and seemed a sure bet to win the race. But just before the finish line, Wade Hampton spied some delicious looking grass. The grass seemed to be too much for the gallant steed, who quickly pulled up short and casually began to nibble away at his prize.

Needless to say, Wade Hampton was hardly one of Clay's favorite studs.

Also in 1845, a devoted friend from New Orleans, Dr. William Mercer, bestowed upon Clay a mare called Magnolia, known as "Empress of the Stud Book," who became, according to Meyer, "one of the great broodmares of her time," with "all of her thirteen foals [growing] to be famous on the turf and in the stud."

An anecdote from the Clay family history illustrates how great her progeny were. One of Magnolia's offspring, Magic, had been entered into the famous Phoenix Hotel in Lexington. John Clay, Henry's son, stopped by a jewelry store in downtown Lexington and noticed that a decorative pitcher, the prize for the winner of the race, was already engraved with Magic's name. John remarked that Magic had not won the race yet. Wasn't the inscribing just a bit too premature? The jeweler responded, "Oh, but she will." And, of course, she won.

Rogers says that Iroquois, a direct descendant of Magnolia, later won the English Derby, just one of the many successful horses that trace their blood to Magnolia. According to Meyer, eleven descendants of Magnolia and

Margaret Wood have won the Kentucky Derby, a remarkable achievement. The most recent are Gato de Sol (1982) and Sunny's Halo (1983).

The third important acquisition that same year was a stallion dubbed Yorkshire, given to Clay by Commodore Charles Morgan. Quickly, Yorkshire proved to be one of Clay's most prized acquisitions. As Meyer says, Yorkshire had showed his mettle in several races in Maysville and "ranked among Ashland's ten leading sires for eight years and sired a number of dams that issued major stakes winners," prompting Clay to remark that "with this great promise of the equine family before you, there is every chance of success."

CLAY RETURNS TO POLITICS

Soon, however, the rush of politics and his advancing years convinced Clay that he couldn't devote the time and attention necessary to fulfill all of the dreams he had for Ashland and his breeding interests. But Clay still wanted to continue his efforts, so he turned over the business to his youngest son, John, a mere twenty-one years old at the time. John Clay's management soon proved to be strong and prescient, as he carefully refined the stock. He was assisted by his wife, Josephine Russell Erwin Clay, who managed the stud farm after John passed away. Another son, James Brown Clay, was instrumental in developing trotting horses, as Henry Clay's legacy of producing only the finest breeds continued.

And while Ashland still stands majestic amidst a grove of trees, it is hardly the breeding farm it used to be. As the years have passed, more and more acres of the original estate have been sold, sprouting modest wood and brick homes. Now Ashland is but an island of a few acres inside the present city limits where once one of America's most important statesmen helped pioneer the world-famous horse industry, where the graceful and mystical motion machines with their elegant and sleek bodies, genetically engineered for speed, still romp in the thick, lush pastures called the bluegrass.

Chapter 9

Fescue:
The Wonder Grass

Kentucky proudly pronounces itself the Bluegrass State, calling up scenes of white-fenced horse farms, verdant fields of green and the pillared porches of mansions with manicured lawns.

Lexington is the hub of this fifteen-county region, with satellite cities like Winchester, Harrodsburg, Danville, Cynthiana and Richmond, among others, revolving around the economic and cultural center of the Bluegrass Region. The rich loam and temperate climate of this area provides bluegrass with the necessary nutrients for the grass cattle and thoroughbreds love to graze. According to local lore, bluegrass has a blue cast to it when it tassels out, giving it its distinctive name.

But growing bluegrass in other areas of the state is a real problem. The remainder of Kentucky, from Louisville south to Franklin and then west through the rest of the Commonwealth, isn't so lucky. Going west, the fertile soil of the Bluegrass Region soon gives way to sticky red clay and other surface soils mostly unsuited for growing bluegrass. And, of course, similar conditions in the eastern part of the state also fail to support bluegrass. In fact, until the 1930s, cattle farmers in these areas struggled to get any grass other than broomsedge and weeds to grow, leaving them unable to provide their cattle and horses with adequate grazing. To some extent, lespedeza worked, but it had to be replanted every two years and then withered when winter threatened, leaving farmers to feed their cows and horses hay for nearly half the year. It was an inconvenient and expensive proposition that quickly cut into the farmers' profits. It seemed like an insurmountable problem, but things soon began to change.

Fescue Is Discovered on Mr. Suiter's Farm

According to a pamphlet issued by the College of Agriculture Extension Service in 1931, Dr. E.N. Fergus, an agronomy professor at the University of Kentucky, drove to eastern Kentucky to judge a sorghum festival. While there, he heard about what was described as a "wonder grass" growing in Menifee County. It seemed to grow almost anywhere—even in poor soils—and it stayed green practically all year.

The source of this miracle grass was the farm of William M. Suiter, who said that he had noticed the grass growing there about 1893, several years after he bought several tracts of land that eventually made up his farm. But it was a neighbor of Suiter, W.K. Wells, who told Fergus about the grass, and Wells had planted it on his own farm from seed he obtained from the Suiter place. Not native to the region, it seemed that through the years, the grass had adapted itself to the rugged soil and climate of the area.

Assisted by J.F. Freeman, Fergus soon accumulated a stock of seed from Suiter's farm and quickly began experimental plantings in different kinds of soil to see if the "wonder grass" was really what Wells said it was. The test plantings all proved positive, and by 1943, the grass was released to the public and dubbed Kentucky 31 Fescue.

But the new kind of grass needed a champion, someone to broadcast the news about its unique adaptation to Kentucky soils. After all, what good was a new grass if farmers didn't know about it?

William C. Johnstone Champions the New Grass

In 1937, an observant William C. Johnstone was driving Highway 66, a couple miles or so before Frenchburg in the foothills of Appalachia, when he spied a patch of green grass growing well into winter on Suiter's farm. It turned out to be fescue, or "Suiter grass," the local county extension agent called it.

As Johnstone tells it in an unpublished manuscript, he had heard about fescue after he had returned to Lexington as agronomy extension specialist the year before, but this grassy field caught Johnstone's sensitive eye because he had just returned from an assignment in the far western portion of the state, in the Jackson Purchase region, where he had tried valiantly and unsuccessfully to help local farmers find a cover that would support cattle.

According to Johnstone, he experimented with redtop, orchard grass and lespedeza, but, as he says, "after many long and problematic years, I found that I didn't have an answer. Grass just would not grow easily in the loess soils of Jackson Purchase. It was either too wet or too dry, and the soils were of low fertility."

Adding to the problem was that Johnstone needed a grass in western Kentucky that would stop the rampant soil erosion that washed away what valuable soil there was, leaving large gullies in the land after "gully washers," frequent storms in the summer that thundered over much of Kentucky.

So after seeing Suiter's farm, Johnstone began his campaign to let others know about fescue—the "wonder grass." He started by encouraging Mr. Suiter to harvest enough seed to fill what Johnstone thought was the demand for fescue in the early going. Suiter, however, was a bit skeptical. But he began gathering fescue seed with a primitive cradle (a modified scythe with rounded wooden prongs), the tool of choice before mechanized combines.

After collecting enough mowed fescue, Suiter harvested the seed by beating out the seed over a box covered with a hardware cloth. He would then fan the seed to rid it of chaff. (It was a less than efficient way of getting large quantities of seed.) He then sold the seed at fifteen to twenty cents a pound.

Johnstone encouraged Suiter to harvest as much as ten thousand pounds of seed. But Suiter told him, "Now, Mr. Johnstone, you know that if we ever saved ten thousand pounds of seed, it would be a drag on the market," not recognizing, as few did at the time, the enormous impact fescue would have on the national market.

Then Johnstone began holding a series of meetings all over the state to prod farmers into planting fescue. By this time, Johnstone was firmly convinced that fescue had a bright future in the Commonwealth. Farmers in Mason County, Larue County, Breckinridge County, Christian County, Carlisle County, Todd County, Greenup County, McCreary County and many more began planting fescue and finding that the "wonder grass" seemed to be all Johnstone said it would be.

But growing fescue was not without its problems. Fescue sometimes goes by the name of "tall fescue," one of several varieties. One of those types was "alta fescue," grown in parts of Washington and Oregon. Seeing a market for fescue, western farmers began offering alta fescue to Kentucky farmers at a lower price than that of Kentucky 31 fescue. But alta fescue wasn't as tough and resistant to the conditions in Kentucky.

Confusion reigned.

CERTIFYING KENTUCKY FESCUE 31

Johnstone and others realized that if Kentucky 31 were to be the grass of the future, Kentucky farmers needed to plant the right variety. To surmount the problem, Johnstone and his colleagues certified Kentucky 31 as the only variety of fescue that was the product of the Suiter farm and the University of Kentucky Experimental Station. Eventually, six hundred to seven hundred farmers were producing certified seed, guaranteed through the Seed Improvement Association.

Seed farmers in Kentucky later told Johnstone that if not for fescue, "they couldn't have improved their homes or sent their children to college." So, certifying seed was an absolute necessity for these seed producers, since to the untrained eye, Kentucky 31 fescue seed looks similar to ryegrass and alta fescue. Today, according to Johnstone, growing Kentucky 31 for seed is a major source of income for many Kentucky farmers.

But farmers discovered other advantages in growing fescue. One plus was that since it often thrived where other grasses wouldn't grow, it became a major force in battling soil erosion. W.O. Gilreath, superintendent of schools in McCreary County and a strong proponent for soil conservation, planted fescue in the sandy soil of the hillsides with so much success that he grazed dairy cattle on the once barren land.

Others across the state had similar success with fescue, saving literally tons of Kentucky soil from needlessly being washed away. One of those people was Dr. H.L. Donovan, at the time the president of the University of Kentucky, who found that his poorly drained and wet soil in Madison County produced enough fescue to turn quite unproductive land into prime pasture while also halting soil erosion on his farm. No doubt his success with fescue influenced the further experimentation and refinement of the grass by university researchers.

In addition, farmers also discovered that when fescue was allowed to grow for a number of years and then plowed under, its extensive root system modified the soil enough that the ground then produced better burley tobacco and corn. The soil that once was too thin to produce anything marketable was now producing crops that could be real moneymakers for farmers.

FESCUE TAKES OFF

Fescue soon became popular in other areas of the South in which the soils and humidity are similar to Kentucky. Seed companies like the Soil Conservation Service in South Carolina; big farmers like the Jones brothers in Huntsville, Alabama; and Atlanta newspaper owner Channing Cope were soon singing the praises of Kentucky 31 fescue. Today, Kentucky 31 is the dominant grass on farms in much of the South.

Kentucky 31 moved north, too.

Like Kentucky, Pennsylvania plants fescue in parks, athletic fields and airfields and on roadsides all over the state. An official guide to planting grass in the state strictly specifies that "under no circumstances should other grass species be seeded with tall fescue. Only blue tag certified Kentucky 31 seed should be used."

Is too much being made over a simple grass? Is fescue really that important?

A couple facts place the value of fescue in perspective. Today, according to government reports, Kentucky ranks ninth in the entire nation in the production of beef cattle, with only states usually associated with large beef production (Texas, Oklahoma, South Dakota, Montana, Kansas, etc.) ahead of the Commonwealth.

In total, Kentucky produces over 1.2 million beef cattle a year, a tremendous number considering the size of the state and the fact that much of Kentucky is so mountainous and unsuited for cattle farms. In fact, Kentucky ranks fourth in the number of beef cattle per square farm mile.

Fescue has to be considered a major factor in these figures.

Considering his many years of experience as a county extension agent and his witnessing the literal transformation of the Kentucky cattle industry, David Cooper of Frenchburg calls Kentucky 31 fescue nothing less than a "godsend" to Kentucky farmers. He has seen how the grass has saved and even enriched Kentucky soil instead of being flushed away into creeks and rivers. He has witnessed subsistence farms that once struggled to support a bare minimum of cattle become significant contributors to Kentucky's thriving beef production, adding to their farm income and helping to feed a nation. He is aware that fescue doesn't feed only beef cattle and horses; the grass is food for a large variety of wildlife, including deer, elk, turkeys, quail and other game birds. He also realizes that Kentucky 31 now flourishes in all areas of the country, where it provides cover not only for agricultural purposes but also for roadsides, parks, athletic fields and even lawns.

A field of lush fescue near Mount Sterling. *Author's collection.*

No wonder, then, that Cooper says, "We ought to call Kentucky the 'Fescue State!'" And in many ways, he is right.

My thanks to David Cooper for his help, Dr. Lowell Bush for sharing the Johnstone manuscript and other materials and Dr. Robert Harmon for verifying government figures.

Chapter 10
The Days the Earth Rumbled and Roared: The New Madrid Earthquakes

KENTUCKY CONNECTIONS

On December 16, 1811, near Fulton County, Kentucky, in the Missouri frontier town of New Madrid, the ground suddenly started to shake—so much so, in fact, that soon, most of the tiny river town had suddenly slipped into the roiling and mighty Mississippi River.

But that wasn't the only devastating earthquake the region would feel before it was all over. In the end, three massive earthquakes, the second and third coming on January 23 and February 7 of the following year, were felt as far away as Washington, D.C.; New York City; and even Boston, Massachusetts. While the scientific study of earthquakes was then in its infancy, scientists today believe that the three powerful quakes would have measured at an 8.0 on the Richter scale, accompanied by three others that measured 7.0 and another ten calculated at 6.0, along with hundreds of aftershocks that shook the ground in the area as late as 1817.

THE POWER OF THE NEW MADRID EARTHQUAKE

After it was all over, the New Madrid earthquakes were the greatest ever to rock the contiguous United States. According to the U.S. Geological Survey, the earthquakes affected over 2.5 million kilometers, compared to about

150,000 kilometers for the great San Francisco earthquake of 1906. All that prevented an enormous loss of life from the New Madrid earthquakes was that the New Madrid area was, at the time, sparsely populated.

The few people present told some strange stories. Reports from the region mentioned the creation of falls in the Mississippi, strange lights on the horizon, fissures in the land, geysers spouting sand, abrupt changes in the course of the Mississippi River and the claim that for three days, the "Mighty Mississipp" ran backward. One eyewitness argued that the quakes pushed his boat four miles upriver, another said the river moved at the speed of a race horse and still another reported that a large hole formed in the river.

In his book on the quakes, Jay Feldman quotes one man anchored near New Madrid at the time as saying, "The sound was in the ground, sometimes muffled and groaning; sometimes it cracked and crashed, not unlike thunder, but as though a great sheet of ice had broken." Another present wrote a friend back in Lexington, Kentucky, and described the sound as a "loud hoarse roaring which attended the earthquake, together with the cries, screams, and yells of the people still ringing in my ears."

While it is difficult to separate fact from fancy, the terror was palpably real to those who endured it. Today, geologists are struggling to try to understand just what happened in the area in the winter of 1811–12. Studying the land formations and using scientific instruments, they are beginning to decipher the code left in the land two hundred years ago.

One of those who worked to explain one of the greatest natural disasters America has endured is Dr. Ron Street, a seismologist formerly at the University of Kentucky. Street argues that the "Father of Waters" probably did, for a short time, appear to run backward in a couple places in the area after the February 7 quake. But he prefers the word "pooled" to describe the phenomenon, concluding that the flow of the river was temporarily obstructed enough in two spots to give the impression that the river had reversed its course.

Yet the earthquakes of the long, terrifying winter of 1811–12 affected more states than others. In addition to Missouri, extensive damage stretched to parts of Arkansas, Illinois, Tennessee and, of course, Kentucky.

THE "BIRTH" OF REELFOOT LAKE

The quake affected Kentucky in some surprising ways. The most obvious way was the formation of the relatively shallow Reelfoot Lake, a twenty-seven-thousand-acre crescent-shaped body of water some fourteen miles long and up to four miles wide that stretches from Fulton County in far southwestern Kentucky into northwestern Tennessee. Besides some of the best crappie fishing in the area, the lake is famous for its natural beauty and the profusion of unique plant and animal life.

Naturalist William Scott names lotus pads with yellow and white flowers, yankapins, duckweed, cypress groves, sawgrass, mulefoot, smartweed and wild rice among the species growing on, in or near the lake. As a National Wildlife Refuge, Reelfoot Lake also teems with wildlife, including wild geese, bald eagles, over 230 different birds and seventy-five species of reptiles and amphibians. Some, in fact, see the lake as a naturalist's paradise.

Local lore has it that the lake was formed when the Mississippi reversed course and backed up into the Reelfoot Creek valley. But some scientists believe that during the quakes, the ground around the lake area sank

An aerial view of Reelfoot Lake in western Kentucky. *Courtesy of the Kentucky Historical Society.*

significantly, damming the existing creek and ultimately forming the present body of water. Street argues that both scenarios could have happened. Relying on historical accounts, Street says that hunters in the area at the time described the land now in the lake as having sunk during the December 16 earthquake, but the February 7 quake could have then allowed the Mississippi to back up into the area of the present lake.

But the lake area has not always been as peaceful as the present surroundings suggest, and at least one of the problems arose because of the abundance in the waters there. Fishermen and hunters in the area who had for years harvested the lake and its surroundings were threatened with the loss of their sources of income when in the early 1900s, the West Tennessee Land Company quietly acquired more and more of the land around the lake. The new landowners then set about to drain portions of Reelfoot Lake and convert the land to growing cotton, denying local residents access to the same land they had fished and hunted for generations.

In retaliation, the local residents organized a group of masked men called Night Riders to defend what they perceived as their rights to the area. Soon, the group turned to violence, terrorizing innocent people, destroying property and eventually murdering five people. The Night Riders took such action, according to a *New York Times* story on October 23, 1908, because "they resented fiercely this destruction of their means of livelihood. Finding no protection from the law, they were ready...to make reprisal by force."

Things got so bad that Governor Malcolm Patterson called in the Tennessee National Guard. All told, more than one hundred suspects were captured, and six were found guilty of murder. But their convictions were eventually overturned by the Tennessee Supreme Court.

Realizing the broad sympathy in the area for the local residents, the land around the lake eventually became a part of the public domain, with access to all, regardless of whether or not they owned land near the lake.

THE "KENTUCKY BEND"

Not far from Reelfoot Lake, on a sharp loop in the Mississippi River, is a small but unusual part of Kentucky, surrounded on three sides by Missouri and one side by Tennessee. One resident said that the small plot of land is the only place in Kentucky where the sun rises and sets in Missouri. In fact, residents of Kentucky can't reach this tiny mass of land without first going through Tennessee. Called by several other names, the most common name for this tract of land is the Kentucky Bend, the lowest point of elevation in the Commonwealth. On a map, shaped a bit like a bud, Kentucky Bend was significantly altered by the New Madrid earthquakes and today includes only about seventeen square miles, with the Tennessee border at the bottom of the bud only about a mile wide.

The result of a surveying error in 1780, the enclave was the subject of a boundary dispute with Tennessee that was eventually settled in 1860 in Kentucky's favor. But according to historian Allen Anthony, as late as 1977, there were still measures designed to have Tennessee annex the area. Specifically, the secretaries of state in both Kentucky and Tennessee, two U.S. congressmen from the area and officials from Fulton County, where Kentucky Bend is located, were in agreement that the area should belong to Tennessee. But, as Anthony sees it, because of the state loyalties of its residents and the power and influence of one large landowner in the region, Kentucky Bend still is part of Kentucky.

Settled in large part by Virginia patricians, Kentucky Bend has its own history of violence. The feud in the bend area between the Darnell and Watson families lasted for over sixty years and involved all manner of murder and mayhem between two supposedly refined families, families who regularly attended the same church together and bore all the markings of a so-called polite society.

What makes this feud more interesting is that it appears to have been at least partially the inspiration for parts of Mark Twain's *Life on the Mississippi* and *The Adventures of Huckleberry Finn*, one of the most significant novels in American literature. Twain, himself a riverboat pilot, records in some detail in *Life on the Mississippi* a conversation he had with an older gentleman who told him about the feud.

Later, in *Huckleberry Finn*, Twain recalls the feud between the Grangerfords and Shepherdsons on his way to deftly satirizing the cult of aristocracy in the South prior to the Civil War. While, as literary critic Loren Davidson observes, it is difficult to say that the Darnell-Watson feud was simply rewritten as the Grangerfords and Shepherdsons in *Huckleberry Finn*, it would also be difficult to say that the Darnell-Watson feud was not a major contributor to the events in the novel.

TROUBLES IN "THE BEND"

Violence of another kind also reared its ugly head in the Kentucky Bend area, only this time it was war—the Civil War, in particular. In the early days of the war, both sides recognized the strategic importance of controlling the Mississippi River, the lifeline for commerce, men and materiel. In fact, the first incursion on Kentucky's neutrality was at Columbus, Kentucky, on the Mississippi River, when Confederate general Leonidas Polk occupied the city in April 1861.

Later, after leaving Columbus, Confederate general P.G.T. Beauregard, commander of the Army of the Mississippi, picked Island Number Ten in the Kentucky Bend to defend the river once more, employing batteries on the island and floating positions of the island itself, all under the command of General John P. McCown and, later, General William W. Mackall.

From February 28 until April 8, 1862, the Union commander, Kentucky general John Pope, dealt with the knotty problem of expelling the Rebels dug in on Island Number Ten. He soon realized that a siege was in order if his forces were to rout the Rebels, so he began a series of moves to force the Confederates' hand. For example, by April 4, his men had completed digging a canal on the Missouri side to avoid Confederate guns on the island. Then, as a diversion, he sent two Union ironclads, the USS *Carondelet* and the USS *Pittsburgh*, to not only occupy the attention of the Confederate guns while he ferried men to the Tennessee side to cut off any Confederate retreat but also to impress the Rebels with the Union's awesome firepower. Eventually, General Mackall, now in command of the Confederates, realized the hopelessness of the situation and on April 8 surrendered 3,500 men.

The Union was now in charge of the "Father of Waters," at least to that point of the river. And General Pope had earned the favor of President Abraham Lincoln, who later appointed him commander of forces charged with protecting Washington, D.C.

THE QUAKES' LASTING EFFECTS

The great earthquakes of 1811–12 had a lasting effect in western Kentucky, not only for the damage they caused to the land and buildings and the cold, bewildering fear they induced in the residents but also in less obvious ways than the rerouting of the Mississippi, the creation of Reelfoot Lake and the reshaping of the land. Aside from their immediate terror, the earthquakes obviously affected the lives of generations of people in that region in ways not immediately apparent.

Surely the earthquakes awakened the scientific world to try to understand their causes and to prepare succeeding generations for what most scientists, if it follows the patterns of the past, see as an event that surely will happen again. One earthquake scientist, Margaret Tuttle, said, "There's no reason to think they won't happen again." With the dense population in the area now, the next time the quakes will surely strike at the very heart of the country and its people.

Chapter 11
Spas in Old Kentucky: Was It Really in the Water?

In the nineteenth century, and even into the twentieth, doctors weren't armed with the vast variety of wonder drugs so common in today's medical arsenal. Without pills, injections, tinctures, surgery, salves and other medications, physicians looked for any means to relieve their patients' ills. Borrowing from a long history of reputed remedies, doctors occasionally turned to water, administered liberally to the human body by both bathing in it and drinking it.

Mid-nineteenth-century America, according to *The Great American Water Cure Craze*, was also a period when all sorts of medical quackery received serious consideration from desperate doctors, but water cures were among the most popular. The water, physicians maintained, not only cleansed the body but also fought all manner of disease and discomfort.

But it couldn't be just any water; it had to be unique water, and Kentucky's numerous special springs bubbled with water reported to cure nearly anything that ailed man or woman. Many of these springs spouted and sometimes gushed out into the green hollows in eastern Kentucky at places like Swango Springs in Wolfe County, Esculapia in Lewis County and Crab Orchard Springs in Lincoln County. But central Kentucky also had its share, including Graham Springs in Mercer County and Keene Springs in Jessamine County. The western part of the Commonwealth included Nally Spa in Union County, Tar Springs in Breckinridge County and Dawson Springs in Hopkins County.

Carlsbad Spa near Dry Ridge, one of dozens of elaborate resorts in which patrons could receive the "water treatment." *Courtesy of the Kentucky Historical Society.*

"The Healing Waters"

All the springs boasted about the miraculous healing that would take place when visitors drank or bathed in their waters. J. Winston Coleman's *The Springs of Kentucky*, for example, cites one advertisement for a spa that promised to cure myriad discomforts and diseases.

In Art Wrobel's article on the springs in Kentucky, he quotes an advertisement for one of the medicinal fountains, Paroquet Springs, that advertised that its water could cure "diseases of the stomach, liver, kidneys, as well as asthma, jaundice, skin diseases, consumption, brain fever, enlargement of the joints, chronic rheumatism, bronchitis, general debility, and female weakness," among many others. The list seemed endless, offering some sort of panacea no matter the disease.

Almost all the "watering places," as they were usually called, proudly trumpeted in all their advertisements an endorsement of a physician. Dr. Donald M. Heard, a "hydropathic physician," for instance, claimed that Greenville Springs's water would have "an exhilarating effect upon the feeble constitution when taken in any considerable quantity…to renovate both body and mind." Many places were even directed by hydropathic physicians, like Dr. C.C. Graham at Graham Springs, known earlier as "The Mammoth Water Cure of the West."

Mineral Springs Spa, near Kuttawa, was especially popular for its "healing waters." *Courtesy of the Kentucky Historical Society.*

Kentucky, of course, was not the only place where hydropathy was practiced. With the popularity of water curatives, most states offered residents some kind of "watering places." Yet all spas seemed in one way or another to be modeled on the elaborate Sarasota Springs in upstate New York. Graham Springs in Mercer County, Coleman notes, called itself still another name: "The Sarasota Springs of the West." All the American spas were in one way or another copied after the baths and spas frequented by the rich and famous of Europe, like the Baden-Baden and Evian-les-Bains, which were largely based on ancient Roman models. Even farther back in medical history, Greece's Hippocrates, the "Father of Medicine," touted spas as places of healing.

Physicians were convinced that the curative element in the water derived from the presence of certain chemicals, particularly one they called chalybeate. Chalybeate Springs in Edmonson County, a popular resort, was thought to possess a highly curative chemical composition in its water. Water containing noticeable amounts of sulphur was also thought to be effective in curing a multitude of discomforts, despite an aroma similar to rotten eggs. Doe Run Springs in Meade County (often called Doe Run Sulphur Wells) featured two wells that spurted sulphur water, remembered by one person as an "almost black" water that "sort of smoked when it came out of the spout." The reasoning seemed to be that if it tasted and smelled that bad, it must be good medicine.

Escaping the Heat

Despite their original intent, the spas soon became less places to get well and more places to avoid the searing summer heat, escape the real threat of cholera and malaria and wile away the summer while eating, dancing, talking politics and finding mates from the elite families of Kentucky and other places in the South.

Horseback riding at Estill Springs Spa in Estill County. Spas featured a variety of entertainment for their exclusive clientele. *Courtesy of the Kentucky Historical Society.*

In the summer in the deep South, when both temperatures and humidity soared to the sweltering upper nineties, landed gentry packed up and traveled to the many watering places in Kentucky, often nestled in cool valleys and surrounded by tall maples and beeches, shading these elite members of the South's upper crust. It was not uncommon to see the affluent families of Mississippi, Louisiana, Alabama, the Carolinas and Tennessee anchored indoors in pleasant surroundings, sipping a mint julep, or under the shade of a tall oak tree, a gentle summer breeze cooling their opulent brows. Coleman says that "these out-of-state guests augmented the large crowds of prosperous and fun-loving Kentuckians who, in most cases, had come to the resorts in stage-coaches, driven by old servants in livery and high hat."

AVOIDING THE EPIDEMICS

These spas also became shelters from what were then the fearful epidemics of cholera and malaria. Coleman mentions that Olympian Springs in Bath County assured possible visitors that "there has been no cholera at this place." Graham Springs in Mercer County did likewise: "These Springs are perfectly free from cholera and they have never been otherwise," adding that "the many who visited the Springs from the various cholera districts, with the disease upon them, have quickly recovered."

In fact, the many deadly cholera epidemics that hit the South in the early nineteenth century were a great boon for business at the various springs around Kentucky, with out-of-state visitors trying to escape the often-deadly disease. Since there was less malaria in Kentucky than areas farther South, the various watering places became safe havens for those from hotter climes, where this disease was a constant threat.

Somewhere along the line, though, watering places became less for curing and avoiding diseases and more like spas, where clients went to enjoy the company of the wealthy. And as the purpose for the clientele changed, the spas became larger and more elaborate to cater to the tastes of those used to the finer things in life. Ella Ellwanger observes that at Estill Springs "on many occasions during the summer months there were over nine hundred guests." Graham Springs, according to local historian Martha Stephenson, could accommodate over three hundred guests at a time. Paroquet Springs in Bullitt County, Coleman notes, held four to six hundred guests. Watering places that catered to several hundred guests at a time were common at the height of the watering craze. So popular were these springs that Coleman lists 122 such places in Kentucky alone.

WHAT WERE THE SPAS LIKE?

The many guests meant big buildings. In Nicholas County, one historian says that Blue Lick Springs was "a handsome three-story frame hotel… six hundred and seventy feet in length, with 1500 feet of 'large and airy galleries.' Included was a spacious dining room, one hundred by thirty-six feet, together with a large ballroom, twenty-six by eighty feet, and 'three elegantly furnished parlors.'"

The same historian records that another resort, Cerulean Springs in Trigg County, consisted of a "three-story frame hotel, with porches on all floors running the entire length of the building, and with bowling alleys, numerous cabins and an outdoor dance pavilion." Stephenson describes Graham Springs as having a long row of "cottages and afterwards supplemented… with a large and costly brick hotel and an extensive ball-room" bordered by stately trees and flowering shrubs transplanted from the mountains of eastern Kentucky.

But these guests needed something to do, and most spas entertained their clients with elaborate and numerous festivities, or "those games and amusements which seem necessary at such a place," as one writer termed them. Stephenson, for instance, lists chess, backgammon, ten-pins, throwing the hoop, riding, walking and delightful promenades. Wrobel mentions masquerades, croquet, horseshoes, shooting competitions, stage productions and, of course, dancing at fancy, formal balls. He quotes one female guest in describing the dances: "We have Germans [a type of dance] in the morning and Balls in the evening." She continues, "A costumer is here from Washington with quite a variety of fancy dresses, most of which have been hired. The majority of the gentlemen, however, will appear in full-dress evening suits." The owner of Graham Springs hired slaves "for the sole duty of playing for his guests." Stephenson notes that "poverty and misery seemed only somebody's bad dream, unthinkable amid hunting and feasting, mirth, and laughter."

Amid this fairy-tale world, it is not surprising that princes would look for princesses. To be sure, many of the planters from down South brought

Massey Springs in the foothills of Appalachia in Madison County. In the summer, visitors often escaped to the mountains to avoid heat and epidemics. *Courtesy of the Kentucky Historical Society*.

their eligible offspring to the watering places to find suitable mates from the assembly of gentry. Stephenson describes how the "belles and beaux walked up and down [the portico at Graham Springs] in what seemed like…a fairy procession."

Ellwanger relates how at Estill Springs, "each tree could tell many tales beside the initials cut deep in the oval of the heart, and if those leaves and branches could speak, the history of the old State would be changed."

Judge John Rowan's daughter from Nelson County writes of her experiences at Harrodsburg Springs, gushing that "there are very few young ladies here besides ourselves and many elegant gentlemen, so you see we are belles from necessity."

Coleman quotes one gentleman who wrote of the many "beautiful Southern ladies who came north with their families to look for romance. Creole beauties from New Orleans added charm and love interest to the great patches of moonlight which shifted down into the spacious grounds. These exotic and dark-eyed beauties, in their muslins and organdies, made the moonlight and roses South a happy reality."

Cerulean Springs in Trigg County, Coleman remarks, was known as "the most fashionable health resort in Kentucky and was described as a 'trysting place of lovers, a rendezvous for romance, a heaven of serenity and a gathering place for graceful belles and gallant beaux.'"

THE SPAS FADE FROM THE SCENE

But the Civil War brought destruction and a decline in business to many of the spas like Estill Springs, Graham Springs and Olympian Springs. Shortly after the war, Crab Orchard Springs, Graham Springs, Blue Lick Springs, Esculapia Springs and Blue Lick Springs were all destroyed by fire. With a decline in business, a number of others closed, although Crab Orchard Springs, Paroquet Springs, Olympian Springs and Rockcastle Springs were revived for a time. New watering places at Stallard Springs, Rock Springs, South Union Springs and Dawson Springs popped up for the first time toward the close of the nineteenth century.

Yet new forms of entertainment, patent medicines, railroad tours like those to Mammoth Cave and Natural Bridge and fewer clientele able to afford the elaborate facilities gradually closed the spas that had become a part of the refined and rich genteel in the nineteenth century. But in their heyday, the watering places teemed with vibrant energy, with the rich and privileged basking in every kind of luxury.

Today, little is left of the ornate buildings with their typical white Romanesque columns, the sick hoping for a water cure, the elegant ladies and charming southern gentlemen promenading the neatly trimmed grounds in search of love and excitement and the elaborate ballrooms with music spilling out onto the lighted grounds—all of which remind us of what Kentucky was like in "the watering seasons" in the gauzy past.

Chapter 12
Salt Making in Kentucky

SALT

The highly respected Mayo Clinic says that healthy adults need between 1,500 and 2,400 milligrams of salt a day. The same source says that we need salt in our diet to keep the body's fluids in balance, to help with the transmission of nerve impulses and to be able to move our muscles properly. So, it's not that we don't need salt; the problem is that most of us consume way too much—not just from the saltshaker but also from processed food.

To the early pioneers of Kentucky, salt was essential. Former state historian, the late Thomas Clark, notes that without salt, many families would have faced starvation. They used the precious mineral not only for flavoring a variety of foods but also as a preservative for curing meat and pickling vegetables.

John Mack Faragher's biography of Daniel Boone even reasons that without salt, the early pioneers would have had to be engaged in "nearly constant hunting [resulting in] a diminished supply of game, wasted ammunition, and increased exposure to attack." So, when the early settlers crossed the mountains or floated down the Ohio River to Kentucky, they were constantly on the lookout for places to gather salt.

Salt was not important to just the European Americans. For instance, we know that the Shawnees valued salt, too. Jerry Clark's book on this Native American tribe mentions that Shawnees may have located

Above: A salt kettle used by Daniel Boone. *Courtesy of the Kentucky Historical Society.*

Right: A statue of Daniel Boone on Eastern Kentucky University's campus. Boone was once captured by Indians while making salt. *Author's collection.*

Eskippakithiki, a large village near Winchester, because of a nearby source for salt. In fact, the Shawnees may also have been salt traders, exchanging salt for other items.

Finding the Salt Was Easy

Locating salt was fairly easy; all one had to do was follow the trail of big game, like bison and deer, to places where salty water oozed out of the ground. The animals licked the salty surface of the ground for their own biological needs. These special spots, called "licks," became the main source of salt for both Native Americans and settlers.

According to geologist Dr. Tom Lierman of Eastern Kentucky University, salt licks in Kentucky formed as a result of a fracture in the rocks below the surface or from an outcropping that allowed the salty water, called brine, to get to the surface. The brine itself came from either the water from an ancient ocean or as the product of a chemical interaction wherein water meets with certain minerals and produces salt.

Extracting salt was a very elementary process. First, salt makers used shovels to dig down deep enough to get at the salty water source. They then collected the brine in large kettles before finally boiling the brine over wood fires until the water had evaporated and left the crystallized sodium chloride (salt's chemical name). Although the process was fairly simple, it was quite time-consuming and left the salt makers vulnerable to attacks from Indians.

Kentucky's Salty History

So important were these salt licks to Kentucky history that the Kentucky Historical Society chose to plant nine historical markers across central and eastern Kentucky to mark places that were in some way associated with salt in pioneer-era Kentucky. These spots include Boon Salt Springs in Floyd County; Brashear's Station in Bullitt County; the famous Blue Licks in Robertson County, the site of a Revolutionary War battle; and Lower Blue Licks in Nicholas County, where, while making salt, Daniel Boone and thirty of his companions were captured by Indians in February 1778.

Thomas Clark points out that during early statehood, possibly the first act of the newly formed Kentucky legislature dealt with the owners of salt licks at the Upper and Lower Blue Licks and Salt Lick. They were required to build a protective five-foot fence of rails or stone around these areas. Three years later, the same body decreed "whereas, it is of the upmost importance to the good people of this Commonwealth, that the owners of salt licks, or occupiers thereof, should be enabled to manufacture salt with as much ease as possible, and thereby have it in their power to sell it on good terms." The law then provided salt makers the right to use wood gathered from the immediate area and the right of eminent domain, allowing them to "convey the brine across land owned by others." In 1810, this same legislative body told the officials of Knox County that they were to build a road from the "salt works on Goose Creek to Hale's place on the Wilderness Road" to convey salt to parts of Kentucky.

A year later, three Slavey brothers were "granted the privilege of claiming 1,000 acres of public land in Wayne County for the purpose of developing salt works," but the lawmakers added a provision that would prevent the three men from creating a monopoly on salt in the area. And in 1815, the legislature made it a felony to in any way interfere with making salt. The law also provided that draining a salt well yielded the offenders a one- to five-year jail sentence.

The early manufacture of salt on a large scale occurred at Bullitt's Lick and Mann's Lick in Bullitt County. According to historian Robert McDowell, by 1779, Bullitt's Lick was the site of the "first commercial salt works in Kentucky—the only salt works west of the Alleghenies during the remaining years of the revolution—and by far the most important source of salt in the wilderness for many, many years thereafter."

According to one source, forty gallons of brine from Bullitt's Lick yielded about one bushel of salt. The industry itself, says McDowell, included elaborate furnaces with walls made from fifteen-inch-thick slate and sealed with clay mortar. Up to fifty twenty-two-gallon kettles rested on a trench where the fire burned and poured its smoke through a large chimney—all under a roof to shield the salt makers from the weather.

CLAY COUNTY: A SALT CENTER

Of all the salt licks in Kentucky, the ones in Clay County were the most numerous and the most productive. In fact, any history of salt making in Kentucky—indeed, any history of Clay County—would have to include salt as a major impetus in the settling of the county, located on the edge of the mountains in eastern Kentucky. Thomas Clark concludes that by 1846, salt making in the county supplied the needs of numerous people within a large area, even into eastern Tennessee.

While the history of salt production in Clay County is interesting in itself, it is also the source of surprising developments. In 1769, the legendary Daniel Boone first located the Goose Creek salt licks but apparently kept that information from others who might be interested in exploiting this rich source.

According to several sources, sometime near the end of the eighteenth century, while following a buffalo trail, a hunter named James Collins stumbled upon a salt spring in the county when his horse began licking a white rock near what is now know as the Collins Fork of Goose Creek. Bessie Hager, writing for *The Register* of the Kentucky Historical Society, says that Collins then went back to his cabin, grabbed some iron pots, scurried back to the spring, boiled the brine and made the first salt in Clay County. It was the beginning of an industry that would dominate life in the county well into the next century.

In *Blame It on the Salt*, Clay County historian Charles House records that soon after Collins returned to Virginia, word of his find reached an enterprising Alexander Outlaw, who quickly realized the potential at Goose Creek. Subsequently, Outlaw bought the land from Collins and then sold it to John Ballenger, who in 1804 sold the land to James White, a wealthy Abingdon, Virginia resident.

The first to make salt was not James White but rather Samuel Langford, at a spot near present-day Manchester, then called Langford's Lick and later dubbed Lower Goose Creek Salt Works. The other early saltworks, the Upper Works, also called the Outlaw Salt Works, followed soon thereafter.

The promise of these early saltworks seemed so bright that the Kentucky legislature proposed a bill as early as 1802 that sought to build a road from Clay County to Madison County. It was a well-founded proposal because by 1850, the nine firms in Clay County were producing 234,000 bushels of salt a year.

THE SALT BARONS

As may be expected, with so much money involved, competition between the most prominent salt-making families—the Whites, Garrards and Bateses— soon led to a climate that fostered a rash of law suits and legal entanglements that tied up courts and generated ill will.

Gradually, such a litigious environment deteriorated into violence. Charles House notes that "the salt men…took advantage of this propensity [among the citizenry] for trigger happiness…and sought to settle their disputes without getting their own hands bloody." Clay County's so-called cult of violence, though, continued into the 1930s long after salt had ceased to be an important product of the county.

Since the salt barons had strong ties with the Bluegrass and Virginia, it is not surprising that these families looked to slave labor to do the hot, grueling work of making the salt. Like the saltworks at Bullitt's Lick, each saltwork contained a series of walls spaced far enough apart to hold the giant kettles filled with brine and far enough off the ground to provide space for the fire underneath. Making salt was lengthy and tiresome work, involving fetching wood to feed the fires and tending the giant kettles as the water bubbled away, leaving the crystallized salt. Slaves mended kettles, constructed barrels and did the backbreaking work of loading wagons and boats.

Economic historians Dwight Billings and Kathleen Blee note that the Whites, the largest slaveholders, owned 162 slaves, while the Garrards owned 37 slaves, most of whom worked at the saltworks. Other families in the county also owned a sizeable number of slaves—James Woodward, for instance, owned 31, and Apperson May held 25 slaves. There is little doubt that salt making in the county was built on the backs of human chattel and came with an economic cost. Billings and Blee note that while using slave labor may have saved the companies much money, it also retarded economic development and severely limited the diversity of industry. The county's dependence on the boom of salt making gave it a deceptively good economic appearance.

Early residents remember the "six horse wagons…from Louisville lined up to be loaded with salt" or the twelve to fifteen wagons that waited overnight to be filled with salt. Another old-timer said that he recalled "a hundred wagons in a train, teams of six horses or three yokes of cattle." To feed and house the teamsters, hotels and eating places dotted the hills in Manchester, with one hotelkeeper boasting that he took in $150 a night, an enormous sum in that day.

THE DECLINE OF SALT MANUFACTURING

Unfortunately, in the end, the salt industry failed for a variety of reasons.

The first factor was the economic depression of the 1840s that hit the entire country. While the salt industry was far removed from the financial engines in the east, the country still felt the impact of a sharp decline in the demand for salt. Salt makers were forced to mortgage their holdings and/or sell slaves, and others demanded payment of some long overdue promissory notes that, until hard times, had seemed insignificant.

Another factor was the persistent problem of transportation. With few good roads in and out, salt had to be lugged on the backs of horses, mules and oxen over long distances to customers. River travel was even more onerous; with few streams wide and deep enough to transport large quantities of salt, boats depended on the spring thaw to swell the creeks and rivers enough to permit travel. Even during high waters, the waterways presented navigation problems when boats were caught in hazardous "narrows" that, at times, resulted in losing a whole load to the treacherous streams.

Still another factor was the discovery of salt mines in what is now the Midwest, where the recovery of salt was much easier and its transportation less difficult than the conditions presented in the hills of eastern Kentucky. As a result, meatpacking industries moved from places like Louisville and Cincinnati, known for a time as "Porkopolis", to Chicago and other points in the Midwest where major rivers like the Mississippi and the Great Lakes provided an easier and faster means to float the product to waiting customers.

Finally, the Civil War also presented problems for salt making in Clay County. Both North and South rationed salt pork to soldiers as a part of their daily diet. That meant that salt was a very important commodity to both the Union and the Confederacy, resulting in a number of military operations with salt as their subjects. Union general Stephen Burbridge, for instance, lead a force to Saltville, Virginia, to destroy one of the South's most productive salt-making facilities. Similarly, despite its Union sympathies, Clay County soon became the target of a Union raid, this time with five hundred soldiers working thirty-six hours to eventually destroy over thirty thousand bushels of salt, denying the Rebels access to this most precious commodity.

John F. Smith, writing about the effect of the Union raid, concludes that after the war, most of the saltworks never reopened, in spite of a promise from the federal government that the owners of the saltworks would be repaid for the damages. The money never came.

Some saltworks in the county limped on for a few more years, but for all practical purposes, salt making in Clay County never again was an important economic factor in the life of its citizenry. With no other industries to support its people after years of dependency on the saltworks, its residents soon relied on what little they could make in agriculture, subsistence farming for most of them.

Few of us realize when we grab the saltshaker to flavor our food, or when we open those tiny packets in restaurants to sprinkle those white crystals on our french fries, just how important salt was to early Kentucky. Still, remnants of its importance remain in our language. We say a man "isn't worth his salt" or that a person is "the salt of the earth." Sodium chloride, salt's chemical name, seems largely insignificant to our lives today, but that certainly wasn't the case with our early Kentucky ancestors, who often depended on salt in ways we can scarcely imagine.

Chapter 13
The Legend of "Devil" John Wright

There is a Letcher County legend about a man named John Wright, known as "Devil" John Wright or "Bad" John Wright. About him, what is fact and what is myth is very difficult to discern. Just start with the name. In some stories, "devil" and "bad" refer to the way in which he pursued his quarry, relentlessly hounding him like the devil incarnate. The lawless shivered with fear at the very thought that Wright was back there somewhere, plotting deviously a way to get their necks in a noose. Other stories say the names accurately describe a man so black inside that he seemed consumed with evil, a man who would resort to any means to murder those innocents who somehow aroused his beastly rage. But Wright also carried a third moniker, "Tall Sycamore of the Elkhorn," a name of neither praise nor blame. With this title, he could be either a quite honorable man or an uncivilized barbarian.

But who was the "real" John Wright? Raging fiend or white knight?

HIS EARLY LIFE

While some parts of the legend are disputed, in a number of areas, some consensus exists. For instance, there is general agreement that Wright was born the grandson of two prominent families in the area: the Bateses and the Wrights. While growing up, his father, Joel, began acquiring more and more

A middle-aged "Devil" John Wright. *Public domain.*

land in the area, property that figured large in the land dealings of his son as coal companies looked for places to mine in what became the economic boon of the latter part of the nineteenth and twentieth centuries. But there doesn't seem to be much accord about just when young Wright entered the world. One source has Wright debuting on May 17, 1844, while another lists his birth date as April 17, 1844, and still another as April 17, 1842.

Whatever the exact date, Wright grew to manhood on land adjacent to the Kentucky River near present-day Jenkins in mountainous and often-wild eastern Kentucky, learning only the bare essentials of an education—six months' worth, sources say. He rapidly acquired the hunting and tracking skills so vital to help feed a family on the game still rich in the hills and hollows, meaning he developed an expert's knowledge of firearms of all types.

Phillip K. Epling's biography says that young Wright "seemed from boyhood to have a natural detective instinct. His eyes never overlooked anything of importance in the field, in the forest, or on the road"—skills necessary, then, for survival whether pursuing or being pursued.

With a tall, sinewy frame belying his powerful strength and physical agility, deep-set eyes that seemed threatening even in casual conversation and a commanding voice that demanded and received attention, the physical attributes Wright developed as a man served him well for ill or good.

Brian McKnight's *Contested Borderland* reports that one day, while young Wright and a friend were plowing, the friend's mother shouted that a troop of Yankees was approaching. Hurriedly, the two adolescents hid the horses, fearing the Union troops would confiscate them. While hiding, Wright witnessed the soldiers "making a general mess about the house." The depredation prompted Wright to quickly join the South's cause.

WRIGHT'S CIVIL WAR EXPERIENCES

Most of those who have tried to record the legend agree that Wright joined the Confederate army at the outbreak of the Civil War, but the question of which unit he joined brings several different answers. One avows that he rode with Lieutenant Colonel Clarence Prentice of the Seventh Battalion Confederate Cavalry with a "mixed bag of Virginia and Kentucky intellectuals, criminals, mountain men and misfits." Another source puts Wright in the Thirteenth Kentucky Regiment under Captain E.A. Webb. Wright, no matter how his age is calculated, was quite young, seventeen perhaps.

The official records say that Wright entered the Confederate Army on October 4, 1862, in Whitesburg, Kentucky, in Enoch Webb's Company D of the Thirteenth Kentucky Regiment. Most sources say that Wright served quite effectively as a courier, carrying messages from commanding officers in the mountains to other Confederate units, mostly in the Bluegrass. Stories circulate about Wright's many encounters with Yankees, who tried in vain to capture the young Confederate mountaineer whose ability to elude his pursuers proved to be too much for those less skilled at horsemanship and understanding the lay of the land.

Wright's years of service must have been quite puzzling. Especially in the mountains, figuring out friend from foe was anything but clear. McKnight makes plain that some Kentuckians joined the cause of the Union while others joined in support of the South, often unpredictably, reflecting their "confusion" over what the war was really about. Few cared about slavery since the terrain of the region did not support any kind of plantation system. In addition, the region was a frequent hiding place for deserters, both Northern and Southern, who formed into small groups of marauding guerrillas that seemed to espouse no cause other than their own desire for murder and mayhem. Some residents often switched their allegiances based on who was causing the most trouble in their area, a way of saying that many just wanted to be left alone.

Such an environment planted seeds of discord that sprouted into various feuds that swept across the region after the great conflict, including the famous Hatfield-McCoy feud. Whether for good or evil, Wright had to reckon with the explosive environment in his own time and his own way.

OFF TO JOIN THE CIRCUS

In the days prior to the war, with the economy in shambles, jobs hard to find and an itch to see more of the world than his mountain home, Wright linked up with his uncle, Martin VanBuren Bates, a former captain in the Confederate army who had grown to an enormous height, some vowing that he reached a height of one inch shy of eight feet, and weighing in at around five hundred whopping pounds. Known as the "Kentucky Mountain Giant," he and Wright became a part of the John Robinson Circus, supposedly an international touring circus.

Wright himself performed as a trick rider and sharpshooter. The legend holds that Wright executed tricks like grasping the mane of a galloping horse and shooting at targets from underneath the animal's neck, "Indian style." He could do the same trick under the belly of the horse. He could also run after a horse, catch it by the tail and bound into the saddle in one smooth motion. He was even reputed to be able to ride a steed while standing on his head—with saddle or bareback. Determining the truth of these claims remains difficult, given the varying accounts by several biographers.

After a time, though, Wright tired of the traveling and "longing," as Epling described it, "for the deep forests, the shaded streams, the lonely cabins, and most of all that feeling of 'home,' which only the mountains of his boyhood could afford him." His days of wanderlust were over.

"Devil" John Wright, Claiborne Jones, Talton Hall and Marshall Benton Taylor: Some Friends and Foes

Almost any account of Wright's life mentions three men who figured significantly in his life in one way or another: Claiborne Jones, Talton Hall and Marshall Benton Taylor. In many ways, the region in which Wright lived was, as Henry Scalf characterized it in his *Four Men of the Cumberlands*, "a locale bordering on anarchy, with rudiments of order held together only by the clan authority of the patriarchs." Wright and these three battled for control, if not supremacy, in such a hostile environment.

Claiborne Jones and "Devil" John feuded for most of their lives. While the nature of their feud is unclear, it is no exaggeration to say that they despised each other. Frequently during their feud, each would raid the other's home and property. One story has it that Wright and his gang and Jones and his group passed one another going in opposite directions, each headed for the other's place on a raiding mission.

Their hatred for each other was so intense that Wright decided to build a virtual fortress to protect himself from Jones and his raiders, a temptation Jones couldn't resist, especially since Jones felt that Wright had moved into his area of authority. Displaying the kind of stealth that an Indian would be proud of, Jones and his followers sneaked up to Wright's brother's sawmill, where the brother of "Devil" John and his employees were working some distance away from "Devil" John. Suddenly, Jones and his men burst out of their hiding and opened fire on the Wrights. Bullets flew from every direction, with men scurrying for the safety of a large tree or a clump of bushes. It looked as though Jones was going to exact his revenge.

Hearing the fire, "Devil" John rushed forward, shotgun in hand, and aimed at Jones and his men. Not willing to call off the attack, and seeing an opening from behind a tree, Jones took aim at John Wright, only to be scared speechless by flying bark from the tree loosened by Wright's shotgun. Jones and his men quickly retreated, but the feud continued.

Talt Hall, an army buddy of Wright's, looked to Wright to hide him from authorities who wanted him for several murders. There were several substantial rewards out for Hall's head, but even when Wright served as a lawman, he protected Hall. What deepened Wright's dedication to Hall was that one of the wounds Hall was suffering from had been inflicted by Wright's nemesis—Claiborne Jones.

But Talt Hall had senselessly murdered Enos Helton, a lawman from Wise County, West Virginia, whom Hall suspected was bent on capturing him, recognizing Hall as a fugitive from justice.

Hall once outlined his defense strategy: "Boys, if he [the enemy] pushes you to fight, just finish him and get away from it. The way to do this is to shoot him in the gut. If it don't kill him, it will at least stop him till you get a chance at another shot."

Wright recognized that Hall was a dead man if he stayed in the mountains, so Wright asked two of his men to accompany Hall to Canada, where he would be safe from capture. The three took the train to Canada, where Wright's men gave Hall a stake of several hundred dollars.

Hall, however, used the money to catch a coach to Memphis, Tennessee, where his spouse was living. Soon, tipped off by local police, Hall was captured and brought back for trial.

So in spite of "Devil" John's effort at trying to hide Hall, which included dressing him like a woman, moving him to a trusted neighbor and paying for an aborted trip to Canada, Hall was brought back to West Virginia and stood trial. He was subsequently convicted and hanged, Wright finally having given up on shielding Hall from justice.

A third person also appears in most biographies of "Devil" John Wright, a physician name Marshall Benton Taylor, generally known as the "Red Fox." Like Wright himself, for a time, the herb doctor served as a lawman, making it difficult to sort out just how much good and how much bad there was in each. One source, for instance, credits Taylor with capturing Talt Hall and bringing him back to Wise County.

A relative of Talt Hall, Big Ed Hall, "didn't like the dual character of [Taylor's] face. On one side was kindness and benevolence; the other was twisted into a wolfish snarl." Another said of the physician that he "would shoot a hole through him I can crawl through, and after he is dead I'll build a fire to hear the grease boil."

Taylor's baser side emerged when he heard that Ira Mullens, an invalid after being shot in the neck, carried a substantial amount of money with him. William T. Wright, one of "Devil" John Wright's biographers, says that after working out elaborate ambush plans, Taylor and his henchmen nearly massacred Mullens's entire family, sparing only one woman and a child. The event, dubbed "The Mountain Killings," was horrendous to locals even in the turbulent mountains at the time.

After several failed attempts, John Wright was appointed to bring in his former friend to authorities. Wright and a scout reconnoitered a cabin in the mountains for several days before surprising Taylor while he was eating breakfast.

Here the story gets muddled. Somehow, Taylor escaped or was set loose in transport back to jail. Scalf relates that Taylor hid out at his son's house before being secretly placed in a large wooden box and shipped by train to the Norton depot, where authorities, who had been tipped off, opened the suspicious crate to uncover Taylor wrapped in a quilt.

Taylor was subsequently brought to trial, found guilty and sentenced to hang. At his hanging, he delivered an extended sermon on how, with Jesus Christ as his solemn witness, he had been betrayed and wrongfully convicted. His wife symbolized his innocence by sewing him an all-white suit with a white hood to shield his face during the execution. Topping off his execution outfit was a brown derby hat.

Taylor requested that after his demise, his lifeless body be unburied for three days, allowing him time to resurrect and again preach to the masses who would hear him. Some are reported to have left a lighted lantern after burial so that Taylor, after recovery, could find his way home in the dark.

"DEVIL" JOHN, THE KU KLUX KLAN, LAND BUYING AND OTHER MATTERS

The legend of "Devil" John Wright also mentions some other areas and matters sometimes referred to by his many biographers. As always, many are highly controversial, with widely differing opinions regarding their veracity.

Ku Klux Klan

While others strongly disagree, some credit "Devil" John Wright with cleaning up a problem in Letcher County involving a band of "youthful reformers" in the late nineteenth century. Supposedly, the group's original purpose, according to one of Wright's biographers, was to rid the county of "lewd women and other evil influences."

Soon, however, the "reformers" went well beyond serving as morality police and launched a series of attacks on the local citizenry. According to one biographer, they robbed the innocent, including Jemima Hall, "an aged woman in the eve of life, with no companions save a grandchild, a neighbor woman, and a chance passerby…The plank house was riddled with bullets, the door jammed with a mattock and the woman already shot to death before the entrance, and then robbed of approximately $4,000."

The community called upon "Devil" John to rid them of the menace that was destroying their lives and livelihood. Complicating matters considerably was that some of the marauders were John's kin.

But "Devil" John was up to the task, and he successfully brought the offenders to justice.

Buying Land for the Coal Companies

When several geologic surveys discovered rich coal seams in much of far eastern Kentucky, coal companies like Northern Coal and Coke Company saw the opportunity for big profits, if they could secure the land. But they also realized that mountaineers seemed to be born with a natural distrust of outsiders. After some investigation, they hired "Devil" John to negotiate the land deals. Possibly, he saw coal mining as a boon to the struggling mountain economy, but he managed to acquire the signatures of several crucial landowners (including himself), providing the coal companies with the properties necessary to begin coal mining.

A few locals felt that Wright had hoodwinked them into selling their land at ridiculously cheap prices, while others maintained that "Devil" John had provided an "invaluable service" to the area by revitalizing and revamping the mountain economy.

The Question of Wives and Children

According to official records, "Devil" John Wright was legally married just one time, to Martha Humphrey from Cynthiana, Kentucky, a woman he had met during the Civil War. However, local reports say that in July 1929, Wright married Ellen Sanders, but no official record exists.

Yet Wright is reported to have fathered from twenty-seven to thirty-five children, surely worthy of a legend in itself. One organization, the Quakers of Yadkin River Valley of Rowan County, Virginia, lists all thirty-five by name, as well as their mothers.

Joe Creason of the Louisville *Courier-Journal* reported that "one of his biggest regrets" was that Wright "never broke even in this life, what with having sired 27 children but having killed 28 men in gun battles."

Indeed, it is entirely possible that "Devil" John himself didn't know how many children he had fathered.

"Devil" John Wright died peacefully at home on January 30, 1931, after having been baptized several months before, an event that drew visitors from all over the region.

But his legend lives on.

John Fox's novel *Trail of the Lonesome Pine*, a classic tale of Appalachia, perpetuates the stories of "Devil" John Wright by recasting him as "Devil" Judd Tolliver in the pages of the work, ensuring that as long as Fox's story is read, people will be interested in the source of Fox's character.

So, what kind of "devil" was "Devil" John Wright? A "devil" to the outlaws or a "devil" to the innocent, ordinary citizen? In the end, how will Wright be regarded? Because there is such wide disagreement about the events in his life, the answer will depend on those who pass on the stories from one generation to another. If they believe the stories to be true, that will shape how this legendary figure from Letcher County will exist in the minds of present and future generations. In other words, those residents will sort out just what kind of "devil" John Wright really was.

Chapter 14
A Short History of Hemp in Kentucky: From Cash Crop to Agricultural Pariah

U p until recently, Kentucky has been known—agriculturally, at least— as a tobacco state, competing with North Carolina as the top producer of burley tobacco. Familiar scenes of rectangular fields filled with light green plants with broad leaves rising several feet in the air during mid-summer are replaced in late summer by stalks resting on three-foot tobacco sticks, forming a field full of miniature mint-green tents awaiting a wagon to tote them to a barn to cure.

But Kentucky's tobacco crop was not always the cash crop on which farmers relied to pay the bills and feed the family. In fact, even into the second decade of the twentieth century, the cash crop in the Commonwealth was not tobacco, but hemp. From 1840 to 1860, Kentucky produced more hemp

From 1840 to 1860, Kentucky led the nation in hemp production. *Courtesy of the Kentucky Historical Society.*

than any other state. And in the late 1800s, ten counties in the Bluegrass accounted for 90 percent of the hemp produced in the entire country.

But Kentucky did not just grow hemp; the state also supported a significant industry manufacturing a number of products from processed hemp, including twine, rope, gunny sacks and bags for cotton bales, just to name a few.

What's the Difference between Hemp and Marijuana?

Much confusion surrounds the question of whether hemp and marijuana are the same. Dr. Ronald Jones, author of the comprehensive *Plant Life of Kentucky*, says that while belonging to the same plant species, industrial hemp, the kind grown in early Kentucky, and marijuana (*Cannabis sativa*) are indeed chemically different. Industrial hemp, for example, contains very little THC, the chemical intoxicant present in marijuana.

Both plants, however, are illegal to grow in Kentucky.

An Early History of Hemp in the Commonwealth

Kentucky pioneers, miles and mountains from clothing stores, had to find a way to obtain fibers strong enough to be woven into cloth to make their own clothes. The Puritans, for example, grew flax, a tall plant that produced enough fibers to make linen. Kentucky pioneers often followed the Puritan lead. Later, however, linen fibers were blended with either cotton or wool to yield a cloth called linsey-woolsey, a popular blend for making clothes of all types in early America.

The procedure for extracting the fibers from the plant was quite detailed and difficult, including allowing the plant to be "retted" (preparing it to extract the fibers) by submerging its stalk in some form of water, usually a pond or stream. And other phases of American life soon convinced these early settlers that a plant other than flax might provide a richer source of fiber.

In the late eighteenth century, the newly liberated United States flexed its mariners' muscles and began searching the oceans for products from the sea, things like whale oil and fish. Ships, however, needed lots of ropes, ropes to set sails and ropes to tie up to docks. What soon became apparent was that industrial hemp was a good source of fiber to make strong ropes for these busy ships.

Yet another aspect of American life also increased the need for hemp. In the Deep South, where cotton was the big money crop, hemp twine was used to tie cotton bales together and to make bagging to put the bales in, profoundly affecting the importance of hemp as a crop in Kentucky.

Credit for the first crop of hemp in Kentucky goes to Archibald McNeil, who sowed the seeds in Boyle County soil in 1775 on Clark's Run Creek, near Danville. But others soon got into the act, too, including the man most often credited with inventing bourbon whiskey, Reverend Elijah Craig of Scott County, who in 1789 established one of the first ropewalks in the state. Ropewalks were, by nature, long sheds of sufficient length to permit the twisting together of hemp fibers to form ropes. By the 1840s, neighboring Fayette County had sixty-three ropewalks.

One of the most famous beneficiaries of the booming hemp industry was General John Hunt Morgan, the famous Confederate cavalry leader in the Civil War.

Numerous hemp factories were also located in Louisville and Maysville, as northern Kentucky's Mason County also had a significant acreage devoted to hemp.

EXTRACTING THE FIBER FROM THE HEMP PLANT

While hemp grew well in the rich soils of the Bluegrass Region, pulling the fibers from the plant was no easy job, which accounts in part for the large number of slaves in the Bluegrass. In 1860, Woodford County, for instance, had the highest percentage of slaves of any county in the Commonwealth.

According to James Hopkins's book on the history of hemp in Kentucky, growers used one of two ways to extract the fiber from the hemp stalk. One, called "dew rotting," involved gathering the hemp plants into sheaves and allowing them to cure for several weeks. Usually in November, workers then broke the sheaves open and spread them out evenly on the ground, where the colder rains, melted snow and frosts helped to break down the natural chemicals in the plants, permitting the fibers to mature into something more accessible. The hemp stalks were frequently turned over for a more thorough "rotting." The whole process took from thirty to sixty days.

A hemp plant in Lancaster. *Courtesy of the Kentucky Historical Society.*

"Water rotting," sometimes called "steeping," says James Hopkins, is "an entirely different process, about which there were many theories as to the best method." In the most common variety of water rotting, workers put the bundles of hemp into running streams, ponds, vats or tanks. Because the sheaves tended to float, some kind of device, usually a frame or weight, was attached to keep the bundles submerged in cold water for about a month and a half. Another variety of water rotting was to submerge the hemp into water at a temperature of 102 degrees. This sped-up process usually took as little as three days until the hemp was ready to be "broken," or extracted from the stalk. Some farmers tried elaborate chemical applications, but these resulted in cloth that rotted after a short time and tore easily.

After breaking the fibers from the plant, the hemp farmer spent considerable manpower processing the extracted fibers, readying them for market by means of a variety of especially designed devices, called "machine brakes," or by hand braking, a slow and arduous process. Harvesting the fibers too soon or too late resulted in a crop that produced fibers of little value.

Water-rotted hemp fibers sold for a higher price than dew rotted-hemp, but few farmers used this method of extracting the fibers because it often required a substantial outlay of money for the operation. Furthermore, water rotting polluted the ponds and streams, making them unfit for fish, and tainted the water that cattle drank. Hopkins also notes that while dew-rotted hemp was mainly used for bagging and rope, its fiber seemed just as suitable and less trouble than water-rotted fiber.

THE DECLINE OF HEMP FARMING IN KENTUCKY

The glory days of Kentucky hemp suddenly came to a halt with the beginning of the Civil War. The Deep South, blockaded by Union ships and isolated from Kentucky by Yankee troops, couldn't buy hemp to make baling rope and bagging for cotton bales. As Hopkins notes, the war "signaled the end of hemp production as one of the major pursuits of Bluegrass farmers." During the war, however, cotton farmers developed new ways of baling cotton using metal and wooden clasps that didn't use hemp twine and bagging.

Amid the conflict, Congress appropriated money to explore the possibility of using hemp instead of cotton as a fiber of choice. But the movement never caught on. Union ships certainly needed more rope for rigging, but by war's end, the demand diminished considerably.

In Kentucky, since hemp growing and production also depended upon slave labor, with the emancipation of millions of slaves, hemp was not the cash crop it had been before the liberation of African Americans. By century's end, one contemporary report complained that growing tobacco was "taking the place of the one-time favorite—hemp—as a money crop."

With the onset of the two world wars in the twentieth century, growing hemp in the Commonwealth was briefly revived. Hopkins notes that during the wars, hemp was used for practically everything from "shoe laces to twine for grain harvest, and calking in ships." But hemp became a money crop not just in Kentucky; Wisconsin, Minnesota and a variety of other midwestern states grew the fibrous crop, too. In fact, the hemp processing plant in Winchester was the only one located in the state during World War II.

Competition from other countries such as India, Russia and the Philippines that produced a superior variety in the minds of those who would have bought domestic hemp gradually eroded the need for American hemp in general and Kentucky in particular.

WILL HEMP EVER BE GROWN AGAIN IN KENTUCKY?

In 1995, a governor's task force explored the possibility of growing hemp and "related fiber crops" in the Commonwealth. Taking testimony from a variety of sources, the group looked extensively at the future of hemp growing in the state.

Acknowledging the many possible uses of hemp products, including dietary supplements, edible oils, building materials and pulp and paper products, the recurring stumbling block was the federal and state laws prohibiting the growing of "controlled substances," including industrial hemp.

While potential hemp growers argued that hemp did not contain nearly the amount of THC, "the proactive narcotic ingredient" in marijuana, according to the report, "some authorities have speculated that fiber hemp with a concentration of .01 to 0.3% would have significant potential for narcotic applications." In addition, the similarity in the appearance of the plants would make it difficult for law enforcement authorities to distinguish between the two.

The commission concluded that "with the current legal restrictions, development of an infrastructure for hemp remains impossible." It further noted that other countries where industrial hemp was grown and marketed had already cornered the market. To be successful, hemp growers would have to build "viable markets" to compete with European countries like Germany and the Netherlands.

At present, the future of hemp as a cash crop in Kentucky looks unpromising. Scientists, through selective breeding, could possibly develop a variety of hemp that contained virtually no narcotic elements, but law enforcement officials would still be faced with the problem of identifying hemp and distinguishing it from marijuana. With modem plant science, however, the day could come when Kentucky might reexperience the hemp-growing prosperity it enjoyed in the nineteenth century.

Chapter 15
Dueling Kentucky Style: The Development of the Caste System in Kentucky and the South

For the most part, Kentucky was settled by people who were economically poor by today's standards. These people came to Kentucky seeking to break out of the economic circumstances that severely limited their incomes and hopefully would permit them to prosper. In particular, the Scots-Irish found that when they landed on American shores, all the good land on the coast had already been taken. So they headed west, many settling in western Pennsylvania and then later moving on to Kentucky, Tennessee and other parts of the rural South. Mixed in with the Scots-Irish were people from England, other parts of Ireland and a few Germans and Dutch, as well as other ethnic groups.

Most of the settlers did find land, but few prospered in the ways they had imagined. A number acquired land in the Bluegrass Region and other parts of the Commonwealth where large farms, generally called plantations, worked with slave labor, tending highly profitable crops like tobacco and hemp, creating a class of generally wealthy gentry. Many had money before they settled in Kentucky, so they could afford the richest land, but others, tilling the rich loam, had to work toward financial security.

Many of this same group were born in Virginia, Maryland and the Carolinas but also came from other areas along the East Coast. They essentially saw themselves as a part of a clearly marked caste system with themselves, of course, in the upper caste. For want of a better phrase, they clung to an idea called "southern chivalry" and what they conceived to be very clear notions of what constituted being a "gentleman" and what was meant by "honor."

THE CODE OF SOUTHERN HONOR

In describing the period roughly from the early days of the Republic up to about the era following the Civil War, Bertram Wyatt-Brown's book *Honor and Violence in the Old South* lists four strongly held beliefs of this group of wealthy land owners and other rich and powerful men.

First was the belief that honor meant "immortalizing valor, particularly in the character of revenge against familial and community enemies." Essentially, if someone speaks ill in any way of you, your state, your town or any member of your family, you must exact revenge in order to maintain the respect of the community or society to which he seeks to belong.

The second belief grew out of the first: the gentleman of honor saw "the opinion of others as an indispensable part of personal identity and a gauge of self-worth." In other words, a gentleman societal reputation was of paramount importance. How people in the upper crust regarded a man was one of the most important aspects of southern society at that time, an aspect still important today in the South and much of the rest of the country.

Thirdly, the code regarded "physical appearance and ferocity of will as signs of inner merit." To say it another way, a gentleman dressed like a gentleman and looked like a gentleman. Men of weak constitutions who showed any signs of effeminate behavior were seen as largely unrepresentative of those qualities of a gentleman: physical strength and a commanding masculine presence. A gentleman must speak in a manly voice, be masculine in physique and wear clothing befitting a gentleman of his economic stature.

Finally, a gentleman must be ready to defend his "male integrity" while displaying a "mingled fear and love of a woman." He must resolutely defend any aspersions that question his honesty while answering any and all attacks on his wife, daughters, mothers or sacred womanhood as it was seen in the South. The old saying that "sticks and stones may break my bones, but words will never hurt me" was not true of a gentleman. Questions about his character or the character of the women in his life were challenges he must defend, even at the cost of death.

At the same time, the gentleman must also realize that women could very easily sully his hard-won reputation by being unfaithful to him, causing those male friends whose acceptance he most desires to see him as less than a man, a man who cannot control his own wife.

The formation of this code was based on a number of different influences. One of those was the classical education that many gentlemen had received. With strong doses of Greek culture as exhibited in Homer's

The Iliad, with its chronicle of daring deeds in defense of Helen of Troy, the exciting pictures of glorious battles that displayed chivalry were all too real to young southerners.

Another important series of popular works were the novels and poems of Sir Walter Scott, who recorded the adventures of knights "in shining armor" during the medieval days in the British Isles. So widespread were Scott's works in the South that novelist Mark Twain once said that Scott was the major cause of the Civil War, filling southerners' heads with notions about chivalry, knighthood and honor.

Wherever southerners got their ideas, they held fast to their beliefs that the South was a very special place in spite of the fact that the sweat of the brows of African Americans was ultimately the source of the caste system headed by white, privileged southerners. Other segments of white society largely acquiesced to the will of those in power, many looking desperately for ways to become a part of the party in power.

One of the rituals that developed out of southern chivalry was dueling, a formalized procedure that gentlemen followed when any disparaging hint of disrespect crept into a conversation or any rumor somehow questioned their integrity. But gentlemen dueled only with other gentlemen; they dealt with lower-class individuals in different ways. If a "non-gentleman" questioned the character of a gentleman, for example, the gentleman would send someone who worked for him—a white man, of course—to deal with the accuser. Or a gentleman would use a whip on the offender, or even a cane, but a gentleman would never challenge a member out of his caste to a formalized duel.

One example of a gentleman dealing with an insult directed at his family actually took place on the floor of the United States Congress in 1856, when South Carolina senator Preston Brooks perceived that Massachusetts senator Charles Sumner had insulted a cousin of Brooks's, also a congressman. Rather than challenging the abolitionist from the Bay State to a duel, Brooks beat Sumner with a cane until the Massachusetts senator suffered injuries that lasted a lifetime.

Surely, what many saw in the North as just a vicious beating was indeed that, but to southerners, the caning was a clear example of how Brooks did not see Sumner as a gentleman worthy of a formal duel.

Wyatt-Brown quotes southerner Lucius Quintus Cincinnatus Lamar, a contemporary of Brooks, who said that if Sumner "had stood on his manhood…and struck back when Preston Brooks assailed him, the blow need not have been the opening skirmish of the war…We are men, not

Dueling was considered a gentleman's way of settling disputes. *Public domain.*

women…Even Homer's heroes, after they had stormed and [been] scolded, fought like brave men, long and well."

THE DEVELOPMENT OF THE DUELING CODE IN THE SOUTH

A number of sources trace the history of dueling to medieval Europe and formalized battles between knights called "judicial duels." According to belief at the time, when there was a question of a person's guilt or innocence, those on one side challenged those on the other to determine who was guilty.

The location of a famous 1806 duel in Kentucky between Andrew Jackson and Charles Dickinson. Dickinson accused Jackson of cheating on a horse bet. *Courtesy of the Kentucky Historical Society.*

Contemporaries believed that God would not allow the guilty party to triumph, that truth would always win out.

In spite of the Church's objections, the practice of dueling for other reasons continued in virtually all of Europe until it arrived in America—especially in Virginia and Maryland—along with the early settlers, who saw dueling as an honorable way for gentlemen to resolve disputes.

Dueling became so popular that the rules for conducting a duel were formalized, producing a number of books and pamphlets that sought to clearly outline just how gentlemen of honor should comport themselves in the contest. One of the most popular guides to proper dueling was *Code of Honor*, written by the former governor of South Carolina, John Lyde Wilson, and published in 1838.

Dueling was a very highly structured ritual in which men of honor followed a set procedure in carrying out the duel. Other segments of society might kick, gouge, bite and use their fists, but men of honor went about the business of settling differences in a more "civilized" way—so they reasoned.

THE RULES OF DUELING

Since a complete discussion of dueling practices would take at least the same length as the various guides, the best way to understand the rules is to highlight the major components of the ritual.

Duels began with what was perceived by one gentleman as an "insult." It may be something as simple as questioning a man's character, honesty or commitment to the southern way of life. Sometimes it involved politics; at other times, it could be over the honor of the family. Many times, the insult could be simple name-calling, but the important thing was that the gentleman perceived it as an insult even though the insult uttered may have been largely the result of too much alcohol. Wilson's guide to dueling notes that "nothing was more derogatory to the honor of a gentleman than to wound the feelings of anyone, however humble."

Then, the person offended, especially in public and observed by other gentlemen, demanded "satisfaction," a key word in any duel. For if the offended party did not obtain "satisfaction," the duel must continue in one form or another. The offended party then wrote a note to the offender in the language of a gentleman that set forth "the subject matter of the complaint," as Wilson says, "attributing to the adverse party any improper motive."

At that point, the challenger appointed a "second," a friend who then took over the duties of preparing for or resolving the dispute. The second contacted the offender, expecting a swift answer to the letter written by the challenger outlining the nature of the offense. The second then made every effort "to soothe and tranquilize" the man he served. At that point, the second normally received a reply from the offender. If he did not, then the offended party was free to "post" the offender. "Posting" refers to the practice of publicly demeaning the opposition in the form of pamphlets, newspaper notices and posters.

Winston Coleman's book *Famous Kentucky Duels* cites words like "liar, coward, poltroon, vile wretch, or slanderer" as invectives that might be used against someone who didn't answer the call for "satisfaction" of the offended gentleman. Obviously, words like that struck deeply in the heart of a gentleman's sense of honor.

As mentioned earlier, one legitimate reason that the offender may have refused a challenge was that the other party may not be socially "equal," for a gentleman duels only with another gentleman. But if the two principals were "equal," the person seeking satisfaction then received a note from the offender in gentlemanly language, not "abusive" or "disrespectful," because gentlemen should be gentlemen at all times.

At this point, the seconds from each of the two parties were required to meet to try to resolve the dispute and avoid the duel altogether. If that did not happen, the seconds then finalized the plans for the duel: where the "field of honor" was to be, when it was to happen and what weapons would be used. In Kentucky, the weapons of choice were dueling pistols, usually a matched pair specifically designed for dueling.

It was customary for duelers to stand facing each other at ten to twenty yards, a distance marked off by the seconds. In Kentucky, the duelers usually stood with their pistols at their sides rather than first standing back to back.

Because dueling was illegal in many states, duelers would often cross a state boundary where the laws were not as punitive or clear. A favorite place for duelers from Kentucky was across the river from Louisville in Southern Indiana. Tennesseans liked to duel near the Tennessee line in Simpson County, Kentucky, at a place called Lincumpinch, the site of a duel involving Sam Houston, a governor of both Tennessee and, later, Texas.

Accompanying the duelers to the "field of honor" were the seconds for each of the principals and a surgeon for each. Many duels were well attended, while others were kept from public knowledge. The seconds usually test-fired the weapons to make sure that both were in good working order. With the faces of their own possible deaths looming before them, many involved in duels called them off at that point, but if no reconciliation took place, the duel continued. After a flip of a coin, one of the seconds called out the signals, counting down to the moment when he said, "Fire!" At this point, each man fired his weapon, and one, both or neither of the principals may be wounded.

Upon reaching this point, one second asked the other if his side was satisfied. If the challenger said that he was satisfied, the duel ended. Otherwise the duel continued until the principal was "satisfied," but if one party was wounded, the second had to inform the other second of that fact.

During the entire procedure, all men in attendance kept a respectful silence, reinforcing the seriousness of the event and the respect for the gentlemen dueling.

TWO FAMOUS KENTUCKY DUELS

Although the Kentucky legislature passed laws against dueling almost from the beginning of statehood, dueling stubbornly persisted. Since men of political influence were the ones most likely to be involved in dueling, the laws were largely ignored.

Those legislators firmly against dueling felt that the only way to limit dueling was to prohibit those who engaged in duels from holding public office. So the present dueling clause in the Kentucky Constitution of 1891 repeats what had gone before: that those who dueled could not hold public office. Yet the Kentucky Secretary of State's office estimates that at the height of popularity in Kentucky and the South, between 1790 and 1867, at least forty-one duels were fought in the state. J. Winston Coleman's book provides the details of many of the most important of these "affairs of honor."

Those engaged in duels during this time represented some of Kentucky's most important political figures, including the nationally prominent Henry Clay (also known as the "Great Compromiser" and sometimes deemed, ironically, the "Great Pacifier"), a man revered even today as Kentucky's most important congressman, three-time Speaker of the House of Representatives and, later, senator. The other principal in this particular duel was the highly respected statesman and Kentucky historian Humphrey Marshall, who, along with Clay, was a member of the Kentucky legislature at the time.

The duel of January 19, 1809, was prompted by a difference in the politics of both men concerning events that led to the War of 1812. Clay introduced several measures in the legislature in support of policies of the Jefferson administration, including an embargo on British goods. Marshall, a Federalist, vehemently opposed such measures, seeing such policies as inevitably leading to yet another war with the British.

A vigorous debate between the two broke out on the floor of the state legislature and soon climaxed with an exchange of invectives, Marshall calling Clay a "demagogue" and a "liar." Clay responded by leaping out of his seat and attacking the bigger and stronger Marshall. After several blows were exchanged, fellow legislators separated the two. Clay then apologized to the members of the legislature for interrupting the proceedings but added that he wouldn't have attacked Marshall had Marshall been a gentleman of honor. Marshall barked back, "Is this the apology of a poltroon?"

The following day, Clay's second, Major John B. Campbell, sent a note on behalf of Clay challenging Marshall. Marshall, quick to respond, wrote,

"The object [of Campbell's note] is understood, and without deigning to notice the insinuation it contains as to [my] character, the necessary arrangements are, on my part, submitted to my friend, Colonel [James F.] Moore." He then added that he knew where they could secure the pistols. The two seconds worked out the details of the duel, picking a date two weeks after the challenge and choosing the Indiana shore across from Louisville as the "field of honor."

On the day of the duel, each man, spaced ten yards apart, held a pistol down by his side and awaited the word, "Fire!" But Marshall missed, and Clay struck Marshall a surface wound in the abdomen. Neither man was "satisfied," so a second round ensued, only this time Clay's pistol misfired and Marshall was again off the mark. In the heat of passion, both demanded a third round. This time, Clay missed, but Marshall struck Clay in the thigh, a serious but not mortal wound. Again, both demanded still another shot, but the seconds noticed Clay's wound and stopped the proceedings. Campbell later wrote, "We deem it just to both gentlemen to pronounce their conduct on the occasion cool, determined and brave in the highest degree."

Clay, seemingly unfazed by the experience, returned to his hotel room and hosted a card party, resulting in Clay's winning a large amount of cash from friends in attendance, adding an additional layer to his reputation as a crafty card player in games of chance.

Clay soon recovered, assuming his duties as a legislator about three weeks later. Clay, of course, went on to national prominence, and Marshall lived to be eighty-one.

Since Clay had "demonstrated calm bravery," the duel with Marshall seemed not to affect his popularity, perhaps even adding to his considerable reputation. He later survived yet another duel outside of Washington, D.C., involving John Randolph that again had politics at its heart.

Another duel involved prominent Kentuckians, Judge John Rowan and Dr. James Chambers, when the two faced each other on February 3, 1801, in Nelson County. Judge Rowan was a prominent attorney and judge, and Dr. Chambers was a well-known and respected physician in the area. Judge Rowan was the resident of Federal Hill, better known as "My Old Kentucky Home."

The whole affair began quite comically but ended tragically. On the evening of January 29, 1801, the two met in Duncan McLean's tavern to play cards and drink beer. While drinking, the two consumed large quantities of the tavern's most potent brew in the course of a game of twenty-one. Prompted perhaps by Judge Rowan's consistent winning, the two soon fell into an argument—not about the card game, per se, but about who knew more about the Latin and Greek classics, then a part of every gentleman's advanced education. Rowan called Dr. Chambers a "damned liar," responding to the physician who thought he knew more about the classics. Chambers then grabbed Rowan and told him that his breadth of knowledge of the ancients was indeed superior. Soon, the tussle turned to blows, but the good judge was so handicapped by alcohol that instead of hitting Chambers, he hit the brick chimney, displacing his thumb but totally unaware of the damage he was doing to his first digit.

Dr. Chambers then threatened to "post" Judge Rowan if Rowan didn't give him the satisfaction of fighting a duel. Soon, the formal challenge arrived at the judge's quarters. Judge George Bibb, a prominent statesman and senator from Kentucky, served as Rowan's second, while Dr. Chambers chose Major John Bullock. Many friends of both parties tried to work out a nonviolent solution to the breach, but to no effect.

On February 3, the principals and the seconds met on the "field of honor" just outside of Bardstown, with the morning fog still hanging thick in the air. Judge Bibb brought two dueling pistols suitable for the event that both parties agreed upon. Major Bullock then gave the signal to fire.

In the first round, Judge Rowan fired first, but both men missed and both demanded "satisfaction" with a second firing. At the signal, both fired, and Rowan's shot struck Chambers under his arm and into his body. All recognized that it was a mortal blow.

Prompted by his obligations as a gentleman, the judge expressed his apologies and regrets and offered to send for a carriage to convey Chambers to a local surgeon, but Chambers was instead taken to his home, where he died a long, agonizing, painful death.

Because of the popularity of the doctor, rumors soon spread across the community. One piece of gossip had it that Chambers's pistol was inferior, while another suggested that Rowan had a "quire of heavy paper" under his clothing to protect him from a bullet to the chest. The duel became a rallying point for the community around Dr. Chambers, and days later, Judge Rowan was arrested and charged with murder. Here, however, the participant's station in life came into play, with a coroner's inquest finding that the popular physician had died of an accidental shooting.

Others who had attended the duel then testified that the duel had been fought in accordance with the code and that both principals "acted brave, gentlemanly, and honorable." So Rowan was then released. Coleman says that "because of the prominence of the victor in this affair of honor, it became one of the most famous [duels] in Kentucky history."

By the end of the Civil War, dueling became less and less popular in Kentucky as more effort was made to enforce the law and punish those who engaged in the practice. The clause in the present constitution is firm evidence that dueling was not only illegal but also grossly immoral in spite of its expression of gentlemanly honor. But dueling also caused Kentucky to lose some of its most important citizens, as many prominent and promising men followed the code that led to their deaths.

One effect of the Civil War throughout the South was that the notions of chivalry departed like smoke from the destroyed cities of the region. In his *Dueling in the Old South*, historian Jack Williams notes that without slavery as the bedrock, the older dreams of knighthood and honor had to give way to rebuilding the South as that region began to industrialize and face new tomorrows. As he says, "Southerners had decided to make a little money along with their honor…The duel had no place in such a setting."

The days of dueling and the smell of sweet magnolias wafting amid the white stately columns of a southern mansion have long since passed, but in some ways, southerners are still quick to defend their honor and the honor of their families, differing significantly from many of their northern cousins.

Fortunately, though, dueling is no longer the accepted way to defend one's honor.

Chapter 16
A Salute to Country Ham

The early settlers of Kentucky showed a definite preference for pigs. Sure, they needed their milk cows and sheep for wool and occasional mutton, but hogs offered many advantages.

First, sows gave birth to a large number of piglets—sometimes as many as seven or eight—all with the possibility of growing to adulthood and providing meat in abundance. In contrast, cows rarely had more than one calf and took much longer to reach butchering size.

Hogs could also eat almost anything, showing no preference for any particular food source. Hogs could root around in the woods and make a meal of roots, acorns and nuts, as well as the corn yielded by the early fields. Slop in the form of discarded food or whey rendered from making cheese were also hog favorites.

Another advantage was that hogs didn't need as much space as other animals. Sheep, goats and cattle usually require expansive fields of grass or similar vegetation to provide the food they need to grow to butchering size, a process that could take more than a year. Hogs could be penned in a small enclosure and fed without requiring broad, open spaces.

But hogs had yet another advantage over cattle and other grazing animals accounting for much of their popularity: their meat could satisfy a variety of appetites, and plenty of the meat could be used in various ways. Their side meat, for example, could be made into bacon. While perhaps not as tasty as the livers from cattle, hog liver was still a source of nourishment for the hungry. In fact, there were many other edible parts of a hog. While not as tasty as ham, the meat from the front legs, called pork shoulder, could also be cured into a picnic ham. The fat from the hog was usually rendered into lard, used long before the advent of vegetable cooking oil. But besides cooking oil, lard could also be used to flavor everything from beans to biscuits to corn bread, staples for previous generations and still popular today with many Kentuckians. In addition, the meat of lesser quality could, with a few spices and preservatives, be made into sausage. The intestines, sometimes referred to as chitterlings, could be eaten or used as casing for sausage.

Even today, remnants of that eat-everything-but-the-squeal mentality show on many grocery store shelves, especially in the South, where many stores carry pork products like pickled pigs' feet. In other parts of Dixie, some even find hogs' ears proper fare for sandwiches.

Besides the meat, at one time, hogs' wiry bristles were used to make certain kinds of brushes. In former times, the hog's knuckles were squared off, polished and used as dice.

But for all the usefulness of the hog, for meat or otherwise, the favorite hog product was the meaty rear legs, which if prepared carefully and cured just right, could become ham. For early pioneers and even today, ham counts as a rich source of protein that, because it is cured, could be eaten at almost any time during the year, including those long, bleak winters, when food for pioneers was scarce. In early Kentucky, finding other sources of meat like venison or elk in winter often depended on sheer luck. But ham was different; it could be stored and eaten at the convenience of the curer.

Today, ham comes in a variety of styles and tastes. *The Country Ham Book* lists Smithfield ham; honey-cured ham; a seemingly infinite variety of European types, including Black Forest ham from Germany; Serrano ham from Spain, British ham, French *jambon de bayonne*; and canned hams from Holland and from many meat packers in the United States.

Yet what most people in the United States know as ham is what experts call "city ham," a moister ham that has been quick-cured for about twenty-four hours with brine pumped into the ham itself. Generally, in much of the rest of the country, a ham sandwich is made with city ham, and the ham served at Easter or Christmas is, in fact, city ham.

So, country ham and city ham are distinctly different in taste and moistness. In fact, most people would not mistake one for the other, for country ham is a different variety of cured pork and a definite favorite in much of the South. Curing country ham, then, often follows many time-honored recipes and techniques passed down lovingly from generation to the next.

The Popularity of Kentucky Country Ham

Kentucky country ham is so much a part of the state's culture that every year at the Kentucky State Fair, competitors among the many country ham producers in the state contend to produce the state's champion country ham. After a winner is declared, the winning ham is then auctioned off to the highest bidder, often garnering hundreds of thousands of dollars for charity. For example, in 2010, the prize-winning ham was bought by a conglomerate of buyers for an impressive $1 million. The following year, the Republic Bank and Trust paid $600,000 for the champion ham. The *Lexington Herald-Leader* reports that Broadbent B&B Foods of Lyon County cured that year's winning ham, which weighed in at 16.9 pounds.

In addition, the morning before the famed Kentucky Derby, the Honorable Order of Kentucky Colonels gather for a breakfast featuring country ham and all the "fixin's" to champion Kentucky culture—which has to include Kentucky-style country ham.

Each fall, two Kentucky communities celebrate Kentucky country ham with festivals. On the last full weekend of September, the Marion County Country Ham Days serves over six hundred pounds of Kentucky country ham, garnished with cornbread and beans, while the fifty thousand

Located in Dixon, Ramsey's is home to Famous Olde Kentucky Hickory Smoked Hams. *Courtesy of the Kentucky Historical Society.*

visitors watch heels flying in clogging competitions; marvel at the car, truck and motorcycle show; amble through the arts and crafts displays; watch the hay bale toss; listen to the Battle of the Bands; and experience a whole host of carnival rides and other interesting exhibits. Yet always at the center is Kentucky country ham, the source of the inspiration of the festivities.

Cadiz, a town in western Kentucky, hosts the annual Trigg County Country Ham Festival. The festival features a ten-and-a-half-foot country ham biscuit, pieces of which are sold and the proceeds given to local charities. Usually held in mid-October, the festival not only features Kentucky country ham but also plays host to craft exhibits and carnival rides, according to local resident Wanda Lisch. But the focus, of course, is on the ham, usually provided by local prize-winning ham producer Broadbent B&B Foods.

Connoisseurs of Kentucky country ham swear that it has a taste all its own, quite different from other varieties of ham. When first hitting the palate, the taster's impression is the intense dose of salt, one of the main preservatives of the meat. Next comes a burst of flavor that makes the taster forget the salt and enjoy the full flavor of the meat. The meat itself is tender—not tough or stringy as most would expect, but moist enough to leave a satisfying taste of flavorful meat on the tongue.

The Country Ham Motel in Bowling Green is a symbol of the meat's popularity in Kentucky. *Courtesy of the Kentucky Historical Society.*

Kentucky, of course, is not the only state that produces good country ham, for surrounding states like Virginia, Missouri, North Carolina, Tennessee and Georgia also ply the trade. As might be expected, they argue that their country ham is better than that of any of the other states.

WHY IS COUNTRY HAM PARTICULARLY POPULAR IN THESE STATES?

Part of country ham's popularity has to do with culture; most people in these states grew up on country ham. However, Norman Marriott and Herbert Ockerman's *The Ultimate Guide to Country Ham* makes an interesting point about the origin of most country hams. They note that originally, "Home-cured hams…are dependent upon only three factors: temperature, time, and humidity." So before the advent of temperature-controlled buildings, generations of people have relied on the favorable weather in these states to cure hams. Other spots may be too warm, cold or dry, but the climate in the upper South made the job of curing country hams that much easier and, in addition, gave the hams their unique taste and texture.

But even within the region, humidity and temperatures varied, and Marriott and Ockerman recognize a difference between, say, a country ham from Kentucky and one from North Carolina.

For example, country ham that is hickory smoked and pecan colored with a bit of sugar probably came from western or northern Kentucky or western Tennessee. However, hams that have a "light mahogany" color to them and are "dry-cured without smoke" most likely originated in eastern Kentucky and Tennessee or western North Carolina.

WHAT MAKES FOR A CHAMPION COUNTRY HAM?

The Country Ham Book cites the exacting criteria employed by judges in all country ham competitions. For instance, judges look for "how and where the shank end of the bone is cut," as well as the "beveled cut of the leg and how the large part of the ham is trimmed." Color is important, too, as the ham should be "reddish pink" throughout. Experts also look for the percentage of fat compared to the amount of lean mean and an acceptable amount of fat even on the exterior. Judges say, too, that the flavor should be a "mellow, aged flavor with a cured aroma when cooked." While the ham should be salty, the salt should not overtake the flavor of the ham itself. Finally, mavens look for "tenderness [and] the amount of force required when the ham is cut."

Again, while the process of producing country hams varies by region, farmers and producers follow certain steps. The U.S. Department of Agriculture says that a country ham must be fresh pork cut from the back legs of a hog and liberally coated with extensive applications of salt. According to *The Country Ham Book*, sometimes to preserve the meat for later consumption, nitrates and nitrites are used to enhance the color of the meat to a rich red. Some country hams are also coated with pepper and brown sugar, granulated white sugar, honey or molasses, a process called "sugar curing."

As noted, curing country hams usually takes place in those months when the outside temperatures hover just a few degrees above freezing, allowing the salt rubbed into the meat to penetrate more deeply, with a re-application of salt about a week later. The salt is then washed off the surface, allowing it to penetrate even more deeply into the meat to again help to preserve it throughout.

If the hams are to be smoked, that's the next step. People who cure country hams from various parts of the rural South use a variety of sources for smoke. For example, Virginia hams are often smoked with hickory or apple wood, but the drier Kentucky hams are sometimes smoked with hickory, apple wood or even corncobs. After smoking, the hams are usually coated with pepper, double wrapped in some kind of sack and hung up for aging, a process that varies from as little as two months to as long as a year. Kentucky country hams are usually left to hang for about nine months.

The table preparation of Kentucky country hams differs in parts of the state. For instance, before baking a country ham, some consumers soak the ham in a variety of liquids to lessen its saltiness. Some, for instance, immerse the ham in sugar water, apple cider or even colas to make the ham more suitable to many people's tastes. Others adorn the ham with cloves, pineapple or a glaze. A Kentucky favorite is the famous Hot Brown Casserole, which includes bacon, turkey, cheese and spices and, in many places in Kentucky, is garnished with a generous portion of Kentucky country ham. In the Kentucky tradition, some don't even bake the ham but instead fry slices of it. The side dishes served with country ham vary and often include greens, fried okra, beans, mushrooms and biscuits. But perhaps the most well-known side dish is "red-eye gravy," made from ham drippings that have been cooked down and flavored with water or even coffee, which is a breakfast and anytime favorite.

So, depending on the curing ingredients and length of aging, Kentucky country ham may be quite different from country ham found in other southern states. But to country ham connoisseurs, Kentucky country ham has a distinct taste found only in the Commonwealth, a taste that sets it apart from other varieties of country hams. To emphasize that fact, many Kentucky producers are careful to label their hams as "Kentucky Country Hams."

One producer of authentic Kentucky country ham is Finchville Farms, near Shelbyville, Kentucky. With nine employees, and using a time-honored family recipe, Finchville Farms begins curing their hams in early December and ages them until September. At that point, the hams reach what owner Tim Switzer and former owner William Robertson Jr. call an appropriate "flavor profile," the point at which the hams taste the best.

Finchville Farms uses a combination of four ingredients to cure their hams: a generous rubbing with salt, a bit of brown sugar (but they are not considered sugar-cured hams), black pepper and red pepper. Unlike many Kentucky producers, they do not smoke their hams but instead cure them in aging stockings in specially designed buildings, providing the hams with an "ambient cure," as the temperature and humidity in the buildings are not controlled. In the Kentucky State Fair Country Ham Competition, Finchville Farm has won an impressive three times.

Kentuckians are a proud people—proud of the splendor and variety of the state's scenery, proud of the beauty and grace of its thoroughbreds, proud of its diverse and fascinating culture, proud of its basketball, proud of its bluegrass music and proud of the accomplishments of its people. And, of course, they are proud of its cuisine, which includes dishes such as spoonbread, barbecue, corn pudding, jam cake, fried banana peppers, fried catfish and the distinct flavor of one of its finest products: Kentucky country ham.

Bibliography

Abramson, Rudy, and Jean Haskell. *Encyclopedia of Appalachia*. Knoxville: University of Tennessee Press, 2006.

Akers, Vincent. *The Low Dutch Company: A History of Holland Dutch Settlements of the Kentucky Frontier*. Copy at the Filson Historical Society, Louisville, KY.

Algeo, Katie. "Mammoth Cave and the Making of Peace." *Southeastern Geography* 44, no. 1 (2004): 27–47.

Blair, Juanita, and Fred Brown Jr. *Days of Anger, Days of Tears*. Morehead, KY: Pioneer Press, 1984.

Chambers, Virginia. "Music in the Four Kentucky Mountain Settlement Schools." PhD dissertation, University of Michigan, 1970.

Clark, Jerry E. *The Shawnee*. Lexington: University Press of Kentucky, 1993.

Clark, Thomas. "Salt, a Factor in the Settlement of Kentucky." *Filson Club History Quarterly* 12 (January 1938): 42–52.

Coleman, J. Winston. *Famous Kentucky Duels*. Lexington, KY: Henry Clay Press, 1969.

———. "Old Kentucky Iron Furnaces." *Filson Club History Quarterly* 31 (1957): 227–42.

———. "Old Kentucky Watering Places." *Filson Club History Quarterly* 16 (January 1942): 1–26.

Commonwealth of Kentucky. "Report on the Governor's Hemp and Related Fiber Crops Task Force." June 13, 1995.

Creason, Joe. "The History of Jenkins, KY." http://penelope.uchicago. edu/Thayer/E/Gazatteer/Places.

Deaton, John H. "The Settlement Schools: Harmful or Benign: Three Responses to Robie." *Appalachian Heritage* (Summer 1991): 45–52.

Duff, Betty Parker. "The 'Quare' Women: Reformers and Settlement Workers in the Kentucky Mountains." Education Resources Information Center (ERIC). http://eric.ed.gov/?id=ED437241.

Eller, Ronald D. *Miners, Millhands, and Mountaineers*. Knoxville: University of Tennessee Press, 1982.

Ellis, Jack G. *Morehead Memories*. Ashland, KY: Jesse Stuart Foundation, 2001.

Ellwanger, Ella. "Estill Springs." *Register of the Kentucky Historical Society* 9 (1911): 45–54.

Epling, Phillip. *Bad John Wright: The Law of Pine Mountain*. Johnson City, TN: Over the Mountain Press, 1981.

Faragher, John Mack. *Daniel Boone*. New York: Henry Holt, 1992.

Faust, Burton. "The History of Saltpetre Mining in Mammoth Cave, Kentucky." *Filson Club History Quarterly* 41 (January 1967).

Fergus, E.H. "Kentucky 31 Fescue: Culture and Uses." College of Agriculture, University of Kentucky, Louisville, KY.

———. Letter to William Johnstone, August 11, 1972. College of Agriculture, University of Kentucky, Louisville, KY.

Field, Thomas. "The Indian Place Names in Kentucky." *Names* 7 (September 1959): 154–66.

Fishback, Price. "Owe Their Souls to the Company Store?" *Journal of Economic History* 46 (December 1986): 1011–29.

Fishback, Price, and Dieter Lauszus. "The Quality of Service in Company Towns." *Journal of Economic History* 49 (March 1989): 125–44.

Fox, John. *Trail of the Lonesome Pine*. New York: Scribners, 1908.

George, Angela, and Gary O'Dell. *The New Madrid Earthquake at Mammoth Cave*. Louisville, KY: George Publishing Co., 1992.

Hatch, Grace M. "The Hindman Settlement School." *Kentucky Magazine* (1920): 385–93.

Henry County Historical Society. *Henry County, Kentucky, 1798–1995: A History of Our Heritage*. Utica, KY: Henry County Historical Society, 1995.

Hill, Carol, and Duane DePaepe. "Saltpeter Mining in Mammoth Cave." *Register of the Kentucky Historical Society* 7 (1979): 247–62.

Hopkins, James. *History of the Hemp Industry in Kentucky*. Lexington: University Press of Kentucky, 1998.

House, Charles. *Blame It on the Salt*. N.p.: Pub This Press, 2008.

Jones, Ronald. *Plant Life in Kentucky*. Lexington: University Press of Kentucky, 2005.

Kelemen, Thomas. "A History of Lynch, Kentucky." Masters thesis, University of Kentucky, 1972.

Kleber, John E. *The Kentucky Encyclopedia*. Lexington: University Press of Kentucky, 1992.

————. *The New History of Shelby County, Kentucky*. Louisville, KY: Harmony House Publishers, 1999.

McDowell, Robert. "Bullitt's Lick: The Related Saltworks and Settlement." *Filson Club History Quarterly* 30 (July 1956): 240–69.

McKnight, Brian. *Contested Borderlands*. Lexington: University Press of Kentucky, 2006.

Meyer, Jeff. "Henry Clay's Legacy to Horse Breeding and Racing." *Register of the Kentucky Historical Society* 10, no. 4 (Autumn 2002): 473–96.

Monastersky, Richard. "The Great American Earthquakes." *Science News* 149 (1996): 362–64.

Nielson, Aimee. "Kentucky Masters Beef Cattle." *The mAGazine* (University of Kentucky College of Agriculture) (Fall 2009): 14–17.

Ockerman, Herbert, and Norman Marriott. *The Ultimate Guide to Country Ham*. Radford, VA: Brightside Press, 2004.

Otterbein, Keith. "Five Feuds: An Analysis of Homicides in Eastern Kentucky in the Late Nineteenth Century." *American Anthropologist* 102 (June 2000): 231–43.

Pearce, John Ed. *Days of Darkness: The Feuds of Eastern Kentucky*. Lexington: University Press of Kentucky, 1994.

Quisenberry, Anderson Chenault. *Kentucky in the War of 1812*. Frankfort, KY: Kentucky State Historical Society, 1915.

Remini, Robert V. *Henry Clay: Statesman of the Union*. New York: W.W. Norton, 1996.

Rennick, Robert. *Kentucky Place Names*. Lexington: University Press of Kentucky, 1984.

Roberts, Joseph. *The True History of Henry Clay*. Philadelphia: J.B. Lippincott, 1904.

Searles, David. *A College for Appalachia: Alice Lloyd on Caney Creek*. Lexington: University Press of Kentucky, 1995.

Scalf, Henry. *Four Men of the Cumberlands*. Prestonsburg, KY: self-published, 1953.

Scofield, Charles. "A Plea for Inhabitants of That Region." *New York Times*, October 5, 1908.

Shifflett, Crandall. *Coal Towns: Life, Work, and Culture in Company Towns in Southern Appalachia*. Knoxville: University of Tennessee Press, 1991.

Smith, John F. "The Salt-Making Industry of Clay County." *Filson Club History Quarterly* 1 (1927): 34–41.

Speizman, Milton. "The Movement of the Settlement Idea into the South." *Southwestern Social Science Quarterly* 44 (December 1963): 237–46.

Stewart, David, and Ray Knox. *The Earthquake That Never Went Away*. Marble Hill, MO: Gutenberg Richter, 1993.

Tice, Karen. "School Work and Mother Work." *Journal of Appalachian Studies* 4, no. 2 (Fall 1998): 191–224.

Twain, Mark. *The Adventures of Huckleberry Finn*. New York: W.W. Norton, 1962.

United States Geological Survey. "New Madrid Earthquakes." http://earthquakes.usgs.gov/regional/states/events/1811.

University of Kentucky. "Kentucky Geological Survey: Iron Ore." http://www.uky.edu/KGS/im/ironore.htm.

Voltz, Jeanne, and Elaine J. Harvell. *The Country Ham Book*. Chapel Hill: University of North Carolina Press, 1999.

Weiss, Harry B., and Howard Kemble. *The Great American Water-Cure Craze: A History of Hydropathy in the United States*. Trenton, NJ: The Past Times Press, 1967.

Wharton, Mary, and Edward Bowen. *Horse World of the Bluegrass*. Lexington, KY: John Bradford Press, 1980.

White, Roy. "The Salt Industry in Clay County, Kentucky." *Register of the Kentucky Historical Society* 50 (1952): 238–41.

Wigginton, Eliot, ed. *Foxfire 5: Ironmaking, Blacksmithing, Flintlock Rifles, Bear Hunting, and Other Affairs of Plain Living*. New York: Doubleday, 1979.

Williams, Jack. *Dueling in the Old South*. College Station: Texas A&M University Press, 1980.

Wilson, John Lyde. *The Code of Honor*. Charleston, SC: James Phinney, 1838.

Wright, William. *Devil John Wright of the Cumberlands*. Pound, VA: self-published, 1932.

Wroben, Art. "The Pursuit of Pleasure (and Health) at Mid-Nineteenth Century Mineral Springs in Kentucky and West Virginia." *Border States* 12 (1999).

Wyatt-Brown, Bertram. *Honor and Violence in the Old South*. New York: Oxford University Press, 1986.

———. *Southern Honor*. New York: Oxford University Press, 1982.

About the Author

Dr. Marshall Myers's love affair with Kentucky began at age seven, when he moved to the now-defunct company town of Oolite in lower Meade County. After high school, he earned degrees at Lindsey Wilson College, Kentucky Wesleyan College and Eastern Kentucky University, along with additional studies at Kansas State University. Ultimately, he earned a PhD from the University of Louisville and took a position at EKU, serving there as coordinator of composition. He has written for most of the major magazines in Kentucky and has also published poetry and fiction, amassing over 250 publications in all. For a number of years, he served as history editor for *Back Home in Kentucky* magazine. His last two books, *Great Civil War Stories of Kentucky* and *Neither Blue nor Gray*, concentrated on little-known aspects of the war in Kentucky. Now retired from EKU, he serves as president of the Madison County Civil War Roundtable and in

2010 was appointed by Governor Steve Beshear to the Kentucky Civil War Sesquicentennial Commission. He has two daughters, five grandsons and one great-grandson.